JEWS AMONG
THE INDIANS

[handwritten inscription with signature]

JEWS AMONG THE INDIANS

Tales of Adventure and Conflict
in the Old West

M.L. Marks

Foreword by
Maynard I. Wishner

BENISON BOOKS
Chicago

Published by
Benison Books
520 North Michigan Avenue
Chicago, Illinois 60611
312/467-5733

Library of Congress Catalog Card Number: 92-81618

ISBN 0-9632965-1-5

Available at special discounts for volume purchases—for sales promotion, fund-raising, and educational use. For details, contact the publisher.

Printed in the United States of America   6 5 4 3 2 1

Book and jacket design by David Doty

Contents

Acknowledgments

I am deeply grateful to the late Norton Stern, editor of *Western States Jewish History,* for suggesting some of the Jewish protagonists in this book as well as for his passion—so clearly evident on the pages of his journal—in unearthing the stories of many early Jewish settlers on the western frontier. I owe a special thanks to the staff of the American Jewish Archives in Cincinnati as well as to all the devoted and knowledgable archivists and curators at libraries, museums and state historical societies in Arizona, New Mexico, Oklahoma, Utah, Nebraska and Kansas.

Deep thanks also go to Harry L. Stern, whose overall guidance as a friend and antiquarian book scholar have been indispensable; to David Doty for his extraordinary skills and taste in graphic design; to Joe Esselin whose friendship and literary sensitivity have added immensely to the book; and finally to Julian Bach who has been a long-time believer in this project.

This book grew out of my deep personal feelings for the subject matter. I am grateful to Mary, my wife, and to my children, Bill, Tom and Pam, for understanding and respecting these feelings. And for that, which is no small thing, I dedicate this book to them.

Foreword

History can be its most fascinating when it records the encounter of disparate peoples and cultures one with another. The variety of encounters Jews have had throughout their history is probably not equalled by any other people.

There were those tribes, peoples and nations with whom Jewish civilization came in contact while a Jewish polity existed in its ancient homeland. The dismantling of the Jewish state by Rome and the dispersion of the people brought elements of the Jewish people into relationships with virtually every other peoples in the "old" world.

Where the encounter involved large numbers of Jews settling in strange new places, adaptability generally meant taking on as many trappings of the hosts' general culture as was consistent with the retention of some sort of Jewish continuity.

What Mel Marks has done here is to trace the paths of seven individual Jews who opted to seek their futures in America's early West. These are not so much stories of a people as they are stories of individuals. These were Jews who sought to make their way in an environment totally foreign to their pasts. How they did so, what they carried with them and to what extent it shaped their adventure in a new land makes for seven fascinating stories.

They, too, helped build the West as we know it.

Maynard I Wishner
Chairman, National Jewish Community
Relations Advisory Council
Past President of the
American Jewish Committee

Even whilst America was a forest where the red man roamed over his vast hunting ground in pursuit of a scanty livelihood by the chase, the Israelite penetrated into the distant wilds and left his memento in the wigwam of the savage. Last year, we think it was, among the Pawnees of the West, that some *tefillin* were discovered in the possession of an Indian, and several would-be antiquarians were sore puzzled to decipher the strange relic of ancient days, as they thought it; when perhaps it was lost by a traveling son of Israel, or stolen from him by his rude neighbors, or it may be that it was the only thing he had left when he breathed his last amidst savage hordes, far away from the home of his early childhood, far from the places where the God of Jacob is invoked in the assembly of his adorers. But assume what you may, you will still have the conviction that "the son of the weary foot" had been there on the plains where the buffalo's hoof makes the soil ring with his measured tread, before civilization had ventured to plant her standard by the banks of the silent Platte or the remote Arkansas, and before the fierce and silent Indian had cause to dread the advance of the honey-bee and the sure-following foot of the white intruder. And now behold where you find the men of Jacob! Go where you will, you will see them...

"What Can Be Done," *The Occident,*
Vol X, No. 9, Philadelphia, 1852

INTRODUCTION

Early on a spring morning in 1983, I was lying in bed in a hotel room in Santa Fe, staring out the window at the New Mexico sky, when the idea for this book came to me. It was a different idea from the one that had brought me to Santa Fe to do research at the New Mexico State Archives, but I knew at once that it was the idea I had been looking for. It had arrived quietly, knocked on the door, and said, "let me in;" and I bid it welcome. This new notion, which just fell into place, was an outgrowth of other notions that for over a year had disturbed my nights and agitated my days.

The book I decided to write would deal with encounters in the West between Native Americans and immigrant Jews in the middle of the nineteenth century. It would be a book about the men who left behind them centuries of Judaic tradition in central and western Europe and came by overland trail to sparsely settled, barbarian lands in the Trans-Mississippi West. What was remarkable about them was not only their ability to adjust to the hardships of frontier life but their adaptability in adjusting to the culture of the American Indian—to trade with them, learn their languages, even to live among them. Jews and Indians! The incongruity of this juxtaposition captivated me. As I lay there that morning, I knew that getting the required material would be a problem, but I would worry about that later. What really mattered was that the right idea had finally arrived.

With only a few exceptions, the Jews who had dealings with the Indians were peddlers. As it turned out, of the seven men whose stories are told in this book, five were peddlers. The two others, Solomon Carvalho, the artist, and Herman Bendell, Superintendent of Indian Affairs, Arizona Territory, were obviously not. Even though the two were somewhat off the track of the others, their experiences with the Indians during the same time span were much too interesting not to be included, for each in his own way was representative of the thesis of the book.

Common to all the Jews who ventured west during this period was an adventurous spirit. They traveled on foot, on mules or in wagons. They followed the ruts of the beckoning trails that led westward, trading with the white settlers, the soldiers, the Indians and the railroad workers.

In 1848, the Jewish population in America was 20,000, but by 1860 it had soared to 150,000 of a total population of nearly 26 million. Once settled along the eastern seaboard some of the young immigrants learned, as Horace Greeley would say, that they could best make their fortunes in the expanding West. The population was gradually drifting westward, and goods in the new expanding territories, even simple amenities like soap, needles, buttons, lace and gingham, were often unavailable to the new settlers. So not only was the West beckoning to these young Jews but their ambitions, they sensed, could best be realized as suppliers of goods—in short, as peddlers. And being a peddler had two big advantages. Capital requirements were small, and there was easy access to inventory, for it could be obtained with the help of relatives and friends in the East, many of whom were already established merchants.

As early as the 1850s, the peddlers began to swarm across the prairie states, selling their wares in small villages, in mining camps and wherever the prairie suddenly became transformed into bustling communities. These young immigrants never seriously regarded peddling as a permanent means of livelihood. Their aspirations were for bigger and better things, like becoming a resident, or sedentary, merchant, or possibly a banker. Peddling was a hard life. For many, it meant walking many miles a day over rough terrain, in good weather and bad, and always with the heavy pack punishing the peddler's body with each step he took. There were also hostile Indians and frontier lawlessness to contend with. Some peddlers were taken captive by the Indians, some were scalped and others were murdered by bandits.

To be sure, these Jews were tough. They were men of great physical and moral courage. They endured hardships that would be unfathomable today to many of their descendants. If they weren't tough when they arrived, life in the West had a way of toughening them up fast.

The peddler was able to survive because, first, he was strongly motivated to succeed in his new life. Second, he was able to adapt, with remarkable facility, to a life of hardship as well as to the modes and habits of different groups of people. And, third, he was able to find economic opportunities, because here, in the developing West, opportunities were everywhere, waiting to be seized and exploited.

It had been my original intention to study thoroughly the phenomenon of the immigrant peddler, especially of those who had become successful in the mercantile business and whose businesses still stand today. I had planned to trace the development of their firms as well as to profile their lives and the lives of their descendants. But that book will have to wait. As I have said, somewhere out in the high desert of New Mexico, that book was ambushed by the Indians.

Call them what you will—peddlers, traders, traveling salesmen or drummers—men of this sort, men who traveled from place to place, had fascinated me from my childhood on. In fact, that fascination had even shaped my life. My father, you see, was himself a peddler. When he died in an auto accident in 1941, the State of Kansas, Department of Vital Statistics, listed his occupation on his death certificate as "commercial traveler." When I was a child in Des Moines, Iowa, and my playmates would ask about my absent father, I would explain that he was not at home because he was a "traveling salesman." The words, "traveling salesman," had such a romantic sound that my friends, the sons of butchers, small grocery store owners and rag dealers, were forced to look at me with new respect. How much more impressed they would have been with a description of my father as grand as "commercial traveler."

My father was not much different from the men who traded with the white settlers in the old West a few generations earlier. But instead of journeying on foot or horseback, I surmise he hoisted his black sample cases aboard the old Pullman cars or, later, carried them in the trunk of his Hudson. Instead of hostile Indians, my father's sternest foe was temptation: that which arose from too many lonely nights spent in traveling mens' hotels with nothing to ease the ache but some congenial cronies and a deck of cards.

I had very little contact with my father while I was growing up. He would write to me now and then on hotel stationery from places that fired my imagination—places like Enid, Tulsa, Wichita, Oklahoma City and Kansas City. On occasion, he would send me boxes filled with clothing—jackets, trousers, and shirts. It was the Depression, and those parcels from my father came in handy.

Undoubtedly, I idealized the life of the peddler because my father's letters from faraway places had fostered within me many romantic notions about the joys of traveling, free as a bird, from place to place, store to store, talking with the merchants; and it made me long one day to lead the same kind of life. The mythology surrounding such a life might have resolved itself had I been in day to day contact with my father. I would have seen him as he was, a man like other men, with his share of faults and virtues, instead of as an idealized figure engaged in what seemed to me a romantic occupation. Even now, in my mid-sixties, the fantasy, curiously enough, still persists. It persists even though peddling, as my father knew it, has all but disappeared, even though merchandise distribution patterns have undergone dramatic changes, and even though the small town clothing stores my father called on are no longer a part of the American scene.

Not long ago I made a trip to Ottawa, Kansas, in pursuit of this fantasy. I wanted to see the site where my father died. He had made a sales call on a Jewish merchant, who was also one of his friends, and was on his way to Kansas City. On the outskirts of Ottawa, his car had been struck by a train operated by a short-line railroad which made just one trip a day between Lawrence and Kansas City.

I hadn't been back to Ottawa since my father was killed. I drove down the main street looking for the store owned by my father's friend. He was the last man to have seen my father alive.

I managed to locate the store, but it was no longer a clothing store and my father's friend, I learned, had died many years before. He had been a man of my father's age, but somehow I had expected things to have stayed just as they had been in 1941—the store to have operated just as my father had seen it, and the proprietor, a man then in his early fifties, to have been standing behind the counter as he once had been in 1941. But I had been haunted by ghosts from a dead planet, and I drove out of town without looking back.

Before coming to Santa Fe, I had spent a fair amount of time doing research on peddlers at the American Jewish Archives. I knew, from my readings, that the Indians were an indispensable supply source for the Jewish peddlers. The Indians provided them with hides, furs, tallow, pecans and other commodities the Jews would then sell to the army camps or ship back to eastern markets. In turn, the Jews were important in helping the Indians assimilate into the society of the white settler, a role the Jews were able to play because of their uncanny knack for learning the various Indian dialects.

Among the Jews who formed close relationships with the Indians, I discovered, was Julius Meyer, an Indian trader in Omaha City, Nebraska, who traded trinkets and cigars for furs, beads, moccasins and wampum pouches. Meyer could speak a half-dozen Indian languages and was able, therefore, to serve as a government interpreter. Meyer was known among his Pawnee pals as "Box-ka-re-sha-hash-ta-ka," which means "Curly-haired white chief who speaks with one tongue."

In New Mexico, the Bibo brothers—Emil, Nathan and Solomon—were also close friends of the Indians. Solomon was a trader and governor of the Acoma pueblo, fluent in the language of the Acoma tribe. He was so trusted by the Acoma that they entrusted to him the power to lease and sub-lease their lands.

Nathan Bibo, a trader, was a sub-agent with the Navajos in New Mexico. After moving to San Francisco in 1889, he became a frequent visitor to Alcatraz Island, helping Indians who were imprisoned there for various alleged crimes against the government. Nathan was able to serve as their interpreter because he was fluent in the Apache, Navajo and Zuni languages. With his help, a number of Indians were able to prove their innocence, and were subsequently set free.

Otto Mears, a railroad builder and Colorado legislator spent his early days in Colorado as an Indian trader and interpreter. He spoke the Ute language fluently.

Beginning in 1860, there were many Jews in the West doing business with the Indians. In Indian Territory, for example, a number of Jews were licensed to trade within the nations belonging to the Five Civilized Tribes, the Creek, Choctaw, Cherokee, Chickasaw and Seminole. In Arizona, Herman and Joseph Levi had traded with the Apaches. The Spiegelberg and Grunsfeld families did business with the Navajos in New Mexico, together with a Spiegelberg relative, "Navajo Joe" Dittenhoefer.

There were also Jewish-Indian alliances of a different kind. A number of Jewish men married Indian women. L.H. Rosenthal secured a license in 1876 to marry Elizabeth Chambers, a full blood Cherokee. A Jewish trader named Friedlander married "Sken-What-Ux," the daughter of a Colville chief. And Solomon Bibo married an Acoma princess and later sent her to the Carlisle Indian School where she was one of its first students.

There was a Jewish Indian chief, one Nahun Blanberg, who lived in Valencia County, New Mexico; and there was Adolph Kahn, a peddler who for three years rode the warpath with the Comanches.

The encounters between Jew and Indian ranged from marital to military to business relationships. However, there were those in the West who looked for deeper connections. The Mormons believed that the Indians were one of the Lost Tribes of Israel; and James Adair, who in 1775 wrote the *History of the American Indian*, also was convinced that the Indians were Jews, offering as a basis for his theory his belief that there was a similarity in the language and speech of Jews and Indians. "The Indian language and dialect," Adair wrote, "appear to have the very idiom and genius of the Hebrew. The words and sentences are express, concise, emphatic, sonorous and bold—and often, both in letter and signification, synonymous with Hebrew."

I myself have since found nothing in either the nature or character of Jew and Indian that draws the two together in any spiritual, genetic or philosophical bond. The only connection I see is that they were at the same place, at the same time, as either friend or foe, at a critical period of our history. Indeed, what fascinated me were the differences themselves, the very unlikelihood of their associations with each other, and the ability of the Jewish peddlers to adapt so readily to such a disparate group of people.

Up to this point, all that I knew about Jewish-Indian relationships had been learned at the American Jewish Archives. Much of it was anecdotal—bits and pieces of trivia, interesting but transient situations that Mel Brooks would have delighted in if he were to film a sequel to *Blazing Saddles*. As much as I was intrigued by these relationships, I dismissed at first any notion of writing a book, or even an article, on the subject. To recount a series of vignettes would lack narrative flow, I reasoned, and would not sustain reader interest once the novelty of the various Jewish-Indian liaisons had worn off. So I continued researching my book about peddlers until that morning in New Mexico when I realized, quite suddenly, that a book about Jews and Indians together might work if the various encounters were expanded and placed within the historical matrix of the unfolding drama of the developing West.

Almost immediately, I began in earnest to research *Jews Among the Indians*. I traveled to historical societies and museums in the states where my father had called on clothing stores, back to Oklahoma and the central plains, back to the very cities from where he had written to me when I was a child.

In the 1860s, a mere sixty years or so before my father worked the territory, Oklahoma was occupied by the Five Civilized Tribes who had been driven out of the gulf states in 1830 by Andrew Jackson to make room for the growing settlements of white men in the East. They were removed to what was known as Indian Territory, where they had transformed the barren land into a rich, agricultural area. But after the Civil War half of the land which had been given to them in "perpetual ownership" was ceded to the government. The central plains, at the same time, was home to the hostile Cheyenne, Arapaho, Wichita and Kiowa, as well as to the more peaceful Pawnee, Ponca and Osage. The government was trying, with a great deal of difficulty, to assign these tribes to reservations in the western part of Oklahoma, to those lands taken away from the Five Tribes. These lands would be known as Oklahoma Territory. It was all part of the government's plan of Indian consolidation in the West.

Although prohibited by law from entering Indian lands without permits, white settlers gradually began encroaching on the lands belonging to the Indians, in defiance of the law. In truth, however, permits were required not as a way to protect Indian lands from the white man but really to protect the intruding white settlers from the Indians. In 1889, with public pressure mounting for more land for white settlers, President Harrison threw open an unassigned strip of land separating Indian Territory from Oklahoma Territory, and in the subsequent wild scramble, 60,000 white settlers stormed into the area, then known as Oklahoma Lands. It was now only a question of time before the Indians, who were wards of the government and lacking the initiative and resources to redress their injuries, would lose their precious land to the onslaught of the western migration.

Long before the white settlers came, before the Iron Horse cut a trail across the prairie, before the Jewish peddlers came, the Indians lived, at one with the earth, in a lush, untrammeled hunting ground all their own, with herds of buffalo and elk to provide them with food and clothing. Theirs was a land where bald eagles freely roamed the skies, or perched like sentries in the trees lining the clear rivers and streams, fully stocked with trout. It was a time when only the screech of the owl or the bark of the lonesome prairie dog interrupted the night stillness. It was a rich land, and it belonged to the Indians. But the white settlers from the East, along with the invaders from Europe, were on the move westward, and progress could not be halted. I could see both sides of the issue, but the injustices waged against the Indians had saddened me.

Things don't always work out as planned. As I got deeper into my research and into some of the writing, I felt my sympathies toward the peddlers, men like my father, blood of my blood, being eroded. I became increasingly sympathetic to the Indians. They had endured broken treaties, broken promises, and, in the southwest, blatant land frauds by non-Indians. It was a fundamental principle of the government that the Indians were simple, childlike, uninformed savages, requiring continued discipline. So under the guise of benevolence, the government was thus able to justify its various unprincipled actions.

Even though my sympathy for peddlers had been modified, my admiration for them, as well as for all the immigrant Jews who came to the West, never faltered. They were strong, courageous trailblazers, laissez-faire entrepreneurs, with a passion for progress, for increased commercial potential. Their dreams were for statehood for the various territories in which they operated. I loved their spirit, but deplored the fact that their success so often had to come at the expense of the Indian.

Two men who had briefly confronted each other symbolized for me the conflict between the Indian and the white man. One was Joseph Sondheimer, a Jewish trader in Muskogee, Oklahoma, who, as he put it, "year after year had waited for the gates of Indian Territory to become unlocked and the tribal walls to be broken down for the entrance of a better civilization..." The other, a special hero of mine, was Samuel Checote, a Creek Indian, who was principal chief of the Creek nation from 1869 until 1882. Checote's great passion was to protect the integrity of Indian lands and to repel the advance of the white settler. He was a Methodist preacher, a farmer, and a Lt. Colonel in the Confederate army, commanding the First Regiment, Creek Mounted Volunteers. To General U.S. Grant, a wartime foe, Checote was "the greatest Indian I have ever met." When he died at age sixty-five in 1884, he was buried near his home in Okmulgee, Oklahoma, then as now the capital of the Creek nation.

I had come across correspondence from Orlando Swain, secretary of the Creek Indian Memorial Association, who noted sadly in 1937 that Checote's grave "has been very much neglected much to our disgrace."

In 1985, I had further research to do in Muskogee, and while there decided to drive to Okmulgee to see Checote's grave. It was a pilgrimage much like the one I had made to Ottawa, Kansas, to visit the site where my father died. I thought surely that by this time, the Creeks would have erected a monument in Checote's memory, or at the very least restored his gravesite. For this giant of a man was beyond dispute the greatest of all the great Creek chiefs.

I drove down the main street of Okmulgee, looking for the headquarters of the Creek nation. It was located in the center of town, a grey stone building set inside a small courtyard. I asked the Indians inside if anyone knew the whereabouts of Samuel Checote's grave. The Indians shook their heads. One Indian woman said that a descendant of Checote lived in Okmulgee, and might be able to help. She made a telephone call, but the relative also didn't know. I thanked the Indians and walked out. As I passed through the courtyard, I saw a marker, erected by the Oklahoma Historical Society, which lauded Chief Samuel Checote and gave directions to his gravesite. I couldn't understand it: The Indians at Creek headquarters had to pass the marker each day yet none was aware of what was printed on it.

I followed directions to the outskirts of town, and pulled my car up to the Newtown Methodist Church. It was located on a country road, a well-kept, white frame building. No one was on the premises. I walked to the back of the church, where off in the distance I spotted a sign, written in the Creek language, designating the site as an Indian burial ground. I could see nothing more than an empty field covered over with a century-old growth of weeds and underbrush. Nothing was revealed but generations of neglect. Somewhere out in that field, with no visible marker on his grave, were the remains of the greatest Indian Ulysses S.

Grant had ever known. I was struck by the irony that I, the son of a Jewish peddler, was most likely the only man to have gone back to look for his grave.

Just like the day I went back to Ottawa, Kansas, I drove out of town without looking back.

M.L. Marks
Chicago
April 15, 1992

Chapter 1

THE 50TH MAN

It was a day the two small Shlesinger children would never forget. It had been a warm afternoon in Cleveland, and their father had taken them to see Buffalo Bill's Wild West and Congress of Rough Riders of the World, starring none other than the great pony express rider and buffalo hunter himself, and featuring the celebrated rifle shot, Miss Annie Oakley. There were cowboys—racing, lassoing wild horses and riding bucking broncos. There was a musical military drill by the Fifth Royal Irish Lancers as well as some amazing feats of horsemanship by soldiers of the Sixth U.S. Cavalry.[1]

And, of course, there were Indians—Indians doing war dances in full head-dress, or racing on their western bronco ponies. There were Indians with warpaint on their faces attacking the Deadwood Mail Coach and being repulsed by Buffalo Bill and the cowboys, or Indians attacking a prairie emigrant train crossing the plains and again being turned back by Buffalo Bill and the cowboys.[2]

Never had the two children, the little girl, Lillian, and her younger brother, Louis, seen anything to equal it.[3] Nothing in the show, however, excited them more than the battles between the cowboys and the Indians; for regularly at bedtime their father, Sigmund, in his soft, even voice would come into their bedroom and tell them stories about the very same Buffalo Bill, and about Wild Bill Hickok and General George Forsyth and the battles that raged on the plains between the Indians and the white men. How those stories had thrilled them. And now the two children had actually seen with their own eyes the re-enactment of their father's bedtime tales.[4]

When the performance was over, the father had taken his children from their special box seats to the tent that Buffalo Bill and the cowboys used as a dressing area. They watched as their father and the buffalo hunter, a tall man with long, flowing white hair and a narrow white goatee, shook hands and embraced. After the two men had finished talking, the father took the children to the tent where the Indians stayed, some of whom had actually fought the white settlers thirty years earlier on the plains of Kansas and Colorado. The Indians made sweeping gestures with their arms and the father was more excited than the children had ever seen him before. It frightened them, just a bit. But then their father smiled and everyone shook hands, and the children were happy to see that their father and the Indians were friends.[5]

The year that Buffalo Bill came to Cleveland was 1897. The man who knew and talked so easily with the great buffalo hunter and the Indians was then in his middle forties, a small, dapper, somewhat self-effacing man. His name was Sigmund Shlesinger, and he made his living as a tobacco wholesaler.

In his quiet way he had become, over the years, a pillar of the Cleveland Jewish community. He gave his time and money freely, as a member of the Hungarian Aid Society, B'nai B'rith and the Knights of Pythias. He was a vice-president of his Temple and one of the organizers of the Cleveland Hebrew Relief Society, the Hebrew Free Loan Association, the Educational Alliance and the Federation of Jewish Charities. Every community has its Sigmund Shlesingers; so to the casual observer, he was just another prosperous, philanthropic Jewish man, working tirelessly to help the less fortunate. And that he was. But there was also a big difference. To General George A. Forsyth and a small band of Indian scouts, Sigmund Shlesinger—or Slinger as they called him then—was a hero of one of the most violent Indian battles ever to occur on the western plains—the battle, September 17, 1868, on the Arickaree Fork of the Republican River, just west of the Kansas line and seventeen road miles below Wray, Yuma County, Colorado.

It took place between a band of fifty Indian scouts, commanded by then Brevet Colonel George Forsyth and a rampaging horde of Cheyenne, Oglala Sioux, Arapahos, Kiowas and Comanches, led by the great Cheyenne warrior, Chief Roman Nose—over 1,000 Indians in all.

The battle on the Arickaree Fork was later renamed the Battle of Beecher Island in memory of Lieutenant Frederick Beecher because it was during the fierce assault on the scouts by Roman Nose and his forces that Lieutenant Beecher of the Third U. S. Infantry was killed.

The battle was vitally important because it was one of a few key Indian campaigns which broke the spirit of collaborating, warring tribes, forcing them eventually to accept the reservation system. Forsyth had taken a long, enlightened view of the Indian problem and of his role as a soldier doing battle with them. It was his hope that the fighting would somehow be justified, that the day would come when the Indians would eventually accept the white settler and the hated Iron Horse and become integrated into the white man's world.[6]

This is the story of one Jew, Sigmund Shlesinger, and of his own very special confrontation with the Indians. It begins with Shlesinger's arrival in America from Hungary in 1864. He was 14 years old. It was during the waning days of the Civil War, and the young immigrant's main concern was how to earn a living in New York. It was simply beyond all probability that he would one day come face to face with Indians, not to mention being pinned down and under siege for nine days by over 1,000 of them.

But destiny had something special in mind for the young man. From his home in New York, where he had a job as a horse car conductor, he was hired as a clerk by a merchant in Leavenworth,

Kansas, and so begins the first step toward his ultimate confrontation with Chief Roman Nose. Shlesinger stayed with the merchant for about a year but soon became restless. The job was not leading him anywhere, and besides there were other communities in Kansas more in keeping with his adventurous spirit and commercial ambitions. So Shlesinger began drifting, first to Johnson City, or Fort Riley, Kansas, which was then the farthest point the Union Pacific tracks had reached. He continued moving farther west, along the surveyed route of the tracks; for he had heard that there were opportunities to make money trading with the railroad workers as well as with the army troops assigned to guard the workers. As new track was laid, new communities sprang up almost overnight along the roadbed; and these bustling, transient communities offered great commercial potential.

Shlesinger was able to find various kinds of temporary employment—as a clothing store clerk, bartender, cook, waiter, mule herder, and as a shoveler for the railroad. It was during this period, while following the construction of the railroad, that he met Buffalo Bill and Wild Bill Hickok. He admired both men. In his later years he described Hickok as being "one of the finest gentlemen I met on the plains."[7]

In the summer of 1868, Shlesinger fell on hard times. There was nowhere to turn for help because he had none of the family connections of the German Jews. Out of money and hungry, he went from army camp to army camp in search of work. During this time, he learned that Colonel George Forsyth, at Fort Hays, Kansas, was pulling together a company of experienced frontiersmen to serve as scouts against the Indians.

The Indian problem had become serious. With the building of the Union Pacific after the Civil War, relations between the white settlers and the Indians had become strained to the breaking point. The Indians sabotaged construction of the railroad and tried to chase away the white settlers. They attacked small communities, killing the men and terrorizing the women and children. To add to the problem, the Indians had come into possession of firearms during the Civil War, and had become proficient in their use. The army realized, as a result, that the Indians had now become fearsome adversaries who had to be contained.

Major General Philip Sheridan in command of the Department of the Missouri at Fort Harker, Kansas, decided that Indian scouts should be pressed into immediate service to seek out and engage marauding Indians. To command such a complement was exactly what Brevet Colonel Forsyth wanted. With the war over, there were few line commands available to competent professional soldiers, and rather than continuing as a staff officer Forsyth immediately volunteered to Sheridan to head up the command.

In August, 1868, Forsyth received the following directive from the Department of the Missouri:

> Colonel, the general commanding directs that you, without delay, employ fifty (50) first-class, hardy frontiersmen to be used as scouts against the hostile Indians, to be commanded by yourself, with Lieutenant Beecher, Third Infantry, your subordinate. You can enter into such articles of agreement with these men as will compel obedience.
>
> I am, sir, very respectfully, your obedient servant.
> (Signed) Colonel J. Schyler Crosby,
> Acting Adjutant General.[8]

Forsyth's knowledge of the Indian was admittedly limited, but what knowledge he had gained he summarized in this way:

> First, that they were shrewd, crafty, treacherous and brave. Secondly, that they were able warriors in that they took no unnecessary risks, attacked generally from ambush and never in an open field unless in overwhelming numbers. Thirdly, that they were savages in all that word implies, gave no quarter, and defeat at their hands meant annihilation, either in the field, or by torture at the stake.[9]

Sheridan wanted Forsyth to start scouting as quickly as possible, so the colonel wasted no time in assembling his command. He immediately signed up thirty scouts at Fort

Harker, and then another nineteen at Fort Hays. There were now forty-nine tough, hardy men, all of whom had previously fought the Indians. Many of the scouts had served in the Civil War and had then settled in the West when the war ended. They had ample reasons to want to do battle with the Indians.

When Sigmund Shlesinger appeared at Fort Hays in response to the news that a scout detail was being formed, the command was ready to march. Since Forsyth was anxious to have his full complement of men without further delay, Schlesinger was taken on, reluctantly, as the fiftieth man, only to complete the detail.

Soldier-historian, General James B. Fry, gave this account of Forsyth's reaction to Shlesinger:

> Shlesinger seemed to be inferior, in all respects unfit for service; a Jew, small with narrow shoulders, sunken chest, quiet manner and pipey voice, and little knowledge of firearms or horsemanship; he was indeed unpromising as a son of Mars, and after forty-nine scouts had been obtained, was accepted only that he might be counted on the rolls to make up the fifty, and thus enable the expedition to start.[10]

The scouts were an organized company, fully outfitted and ready for the field five days from the time Forsyth received his directive from the adjutant general. Each scout was equipped with a Spencer repeating rifle, a colt revolver, 140 rounds of rifle ammunition and thirty rounds of revolver ammunition. In addition, each scout carried seven days' of cooked rations in his haversack.

On August 29, Sheridan ordered Forsyth to move across the headwaters of the Solomon River to Beaver Creek, and then to follow the creek northwest to Fort Wallace, Kansas. Immediately, Forsyth led his company out of Fort Hays for the Solomon, leaving civilization behind. The scouts picked up the trail to Fort Wallace, but during the first day's ride Shlesinger, not being used to horse or saddle, had his share of problems—a raw backside, continually shifting equipment and a cramped bridle arm. Every muscle in his body ached. When the party reached its first night's camp, Shlesinger was exhausted, too tired to eat. All he could think of was sleep, but it was not to be. He was immediately detailed for guard duty. However, with each succeeding day on the trail, the young immigrant gradually became more accustomed to his mount, and by the time the scouts reached Fort Wallace, eight days later, Shlesinger had become a seasoned horseman.

Shlesinger was not well accepted by most of the scouts. Because of his lack of experience, his youth and his fragile build, he was either coolly disregarded or else the subject of derision. Being Jewish did not help matters. He handled the ridicule by detaching himself from it, and went about his duties. Only two scouts, however, treated him warmly and with good fellowship. They were Jack Stillwell and Jack Peate, young men around Shlesinger's age.

When the command reached Fort Wallace, Forsyth received word that the Indians were on the warpath. They had attacked a freighter train near the fort, leaving two freighters dead. The scouts assembled quickly and rode after the Indians, but by the following day had lost the trail. Nevertheless, they continued on their mission, and within a few days had picked up the trail of a few Indian horses, thanks to head scout Sharp Glover, himself an Indian. As they followed the trail it gradually became wider until eventually it was broad and well-trampled with hoof-tracks. Still, no one in the command had seen an Indian.

Continuing their traveling, the scouts now noticed that the hoof-tracks had suddenly become fewer, as if riders were dropping off from time to time from the main body of horsemen. Scout Glover concluded that the Indians had seen the scouts, were aware that they were being followed, and were observing from cover every move the scouts made.

The scouts continued following what by now was an ever-narrowing trail, which finally led them into the middle fork of the Republican River, the Arickaree Fork. It was ominously quiet. Despite his misgivings, Forsyth was determined to engage any war party, no matter how outnumbered his scouts might be. Whatever the cost, the enormous damage being done to the settlers had to stop.

The evening of September 16, the scouts made camp on the grassy banks of the river in a large meadow which tapered gently down to the edge of the water. Close to the bank was a small, sandy island, a sandbar. On the scouts' opposite flank was a bluff overlooking the meadow where they camped.

After their horses were tied down and guards posted, the scouts ate a little of their dwindling food supply and then retired for the night. They had come about 150 miles since leaving Fort Wallace, but despite their weariness had slept uneasily. The utter stillness of the night was menacing, and the quiet, coupled with the suspicious absence of Indians since they left the fort, carried only grim promises for the frontiersmen. Each man felt the presence of Indians somewhere close by in the Colorado darkness.

Their apprehension proved to be justified. As dawn broke on September 17, Shlesinger was awakened by someone shouting, "Indians!" The word "Indian" came down on him like a death blow; he felt his head reeling. He had never been more frightened. Indians, perhaps a dozen of them, were stampeding the scouts' horses. Moments later, Shlesinger looked up and saw on the horizon an army of Indians, over 1,000 of them, thundering toward him, their ponies in full gallop, their lances festooned with brightly colored streamers.

Now the Indians came closer, their rifle fire coming from all directions. Shlesinger heard Forsyth in desperation give the command to fall back to the sandbar. Scrambling furiously, the scouts clawed their way onto the sandy island while the colonel, barking out directions, strategically positioned the scouts for battle. The frontiersmen now began digging frantically in the sand with their hands, trying to fashion shelter pits deep enough for protection. Suddenly, Shlesinger heard the colonel cry out in pain. Forsyth had taken a bullet in the left knee, another in his right thigh. Meanwhile, the attack continued for what seemed to Shlesinger like hours. In truth, however, the assault was over quickly. His hands shaking, the young immigrant had managed to fire off several rounds at the attackers, and felt surprised at his outward calm in the crisis.

The first assault over, the Indians now withdrew to prepare for another charge. During the attack, the scouts sustained costly casualties. Lieutenant Beecher was killed.[11] Acting surgeon J. H. Mooers was shot in the head, a wound which would prove fatal three days later. In addition, all the scouts' horses were killed. Forsyth, despite being wounded, was still able to command.

Later in the morning, as expected, the Indians returned. By now, the initial shock of the first attack had worn off, and Shlesinger and the others, from their shelter pits, were able to draw their beads on the Indians and hold them off with careful sharpshooting.

Fate had surely decreed a confrontation between Shlesinger and Roman Nose, and now it was at hand. From his shelter pit, Shlesinger saw the Indian leader. There was no mistaking him. Riding defiantly at high speed, back and forth in front of his warriors, was the great Cheyenne fighter, an Indian of gigantic stature, mounted on a magnificent chestnut horse, and naked except for a bright sash around his waist, the moccasins on his feet and a war bonnet so ornate it dazzled the eye. His face was streaked with war paint, and as he rode, fully exposed to the scouts, he waved his arms in a frenzy, shouting encouragement to his warriors, taunting the scouts, defying death; while behind him, strangely, came the martial notes of an artillery bugle.[12] Then suddenly, almost as though he expected it to happen, the great chief's horse reared and mighty Roman Nose went down, a victim of a scout's bullet.

Sharp Glover identified the Indians as the Northern Cheyenne, the Oglala and Brule Sioux, along with a number of renegade tribes. Roman Nose was in command of all the tribes, but other tribal chiefs participated in the battle, among them Big Mouth, Tall Bull, Yellow Bear, Minnimmuck, and Little Robe. After Roman Nose was killed, Minnimmuck, a younger chief, assumed command.

By nightfall of September 17, the scouts realized the gravity of their situation. They were so heavily outnumbered that survival appeared hopeless. Forsyth, now in great pain from his wounds, asked for volunteers to return to Fort Wallace for help. It was the only chance the scouts had. Shlesinger's friend, Jack Stillwell, was first to volunteer. He chose as his partner an older scout, a trapper named Pierre Trudeau, and the two set out on foot for Fort Wallace the night of September 17.

The following day, the Indians mounted another attack. But Forsyth's men hung on and managed to repulse the attack, holding their casualties to a minimum. By now, however, all food was gone and ammunition was running low. The scouts were afraid that Stillwell and Trudeau would not make it safely to Fort Wallace, so Forsyth, now growing weaker, decided the night of September 19 to dispatch two more scouts to the fort. Unfortunately, they were spotted by the Indians and forced to return. Now all their hopes for rescue depended on Stillwell and Trudeau.

It was now September 22. After managing to stave off one attack after another, the scouts had all but given up hope. They were discouraged, disorganized, hungry and thirsty. They boiled the carcasses of their dead horses, salting the flesh with gunpowder to try to make the flesh edible, but to no avail. The carcasses could not be eaten.

As the hours and days wore on, the scouts could only lie in their shelter pits, half-dozing, too weak to offer any strong resistance. Forsyth was now running a high fever, and too ill to encourage his troops. However, the Indians too were having their difficulties. With Roman Nose, their strong leader, dead, there was no longer a unifying force to pull together the various collaborating tribes, and it cost the Indians their fighting spirit. Each successive attack lost some of its ferocity.

In the meantime, traveling only at night, Stillwell and Trudeau arrived at Fort Wallace. They had managed to get to Cheyenne Wells, the stage coach station about thirty miles from the fort. From there they rode the stage to Fort Wallace. It had taken them five days, and during the journey they had managed to get past several parties of Indians.

The fortunes of the embattled frontiersmen suddenly changed

for the better. Three days after Stillwell and Trudeau reached Fort Wallace, a troop of the 10th Cavalry under Colonel L. H. Carpenter rescued the scouts.[13] The Indians had spotted the Carpenter relief party before Forsyth, but by this time the Indians were too demoralized to offer any resistance. The battle on the Arickaree Fork was over. The bedraggled scouts had survived nine days of bitter siege. Nearly half of the complement were casualties—five killed, sixteen wounded. Colonel Forsyth would recover fully, but it would take nearly two years.

The scouts had one coward among them. His name was Whalen. Forsyth made this comparison between Whalen and Shlesinger:

> Only one man in my command had failed me...he had joined the command at Fort Hays, and I was much impressed by his appearance. No one seemed to know him as he was a recent arrival at the post...tall, well-built, brown hair and black eyes, a flowing beard midway to his waist, well-mounted on his own horse, a good rider and with a pleasing address, he not only impressed me favorably but others as well. On our first scout from Fort Hays to Fort Wallace he spoke of several Indian engagements in the far north in which he had taken part, and so won upon me by his statements and general bearing that I thought him, for this especial service, quite invaluable. Something of a joker, he was inclined to guy and poke fun at some of the odd characters of the command and especially at a young Jew of about 19 or 20 who had enrolled just at the last moment at Fort Hayes to complete the complement of 50 men.
>
> He was a short...rather awkward and boyish young fellow with cherry cheeks and verdant in some ways, and entirely new to campaigning, but I soon noticed his good care of his horse, his strict obedience to orders, and his evident anxiety to learn his duty and do it. Furthermore, my experience with men of his race during the Civil War, with a single exception, had strongly impressed me in their favor as being brave men and good soldiers. Imagine my surprise and astonishment, therefore, to discover that my fine looking scout was an absolute failure and coward, while as

for the little Jew...! well, the Indian that from dawn to dusk
was incautious enough to expose any part of his person
within the range of his rifle had no cause to complain of a
want of marked attention on the part of that brave and
active young Israelite...in fact, he most worthily proved
himself a gallant soldier among brave men.[14]

In addition to praising Shlesinger for his bravery under fire,
Forsyth also credited Shlesinger with the feat of scalping three
Indians during the fifth day of the attack, and then again
credited him for killing the coyote which served as sustenance
for the pinned-down scouts.

Shlesinger kept a diary which did
not come to light until 1951. It had been in the possession of his
daughter, Lillian. In none of the accounts of the battle had it ever
been mentioned that the young scout kept a battlefield diary,
and while it adds very little to the historians' knowledge of the
battle, it does give the reader an understanding of the simple
courage of the young immigrant.

The diary covers the period from August 28 to September 22,
1868, and is contained in a notebook 3½ x 8 inches in size. The
entries are concise and filled with misspellings. The most interesting entries begin the night before the battle (see illustration):

September 16: Seen signal fire on Hill 3 miles off in evening
late.

September 17: About 12 Indians carched on us stampeedet 7
horse. 10 minute after about 600 Indians attacket us. Kilt
Beecher, Culver and Wilson. Woundet 19 Man and Kilt all
the horses. We was without Grubb and water all day. Dug
holes in the sand with our hands.

September 18: In the night I dug my hole deeper. Cut off
meat of the horses and hung it up on bushes. Indians made
a charge at us at Day Brake but retreatet. Kept Shooting
nearly all day they put up a White Flag. Left us at 9 O'Clock
in the evening. Raind all night.

September 19: The Indians came back again. Kept sharp-shooting all day. Two boys startet for Fort Wallace. Raind all night.

September 20: Dr. Moore died last night. Raining part of the Day. Snow about 1 inches thick. Indians kept sharpshooting.

September 21: Scalpt 3 Indians which were found about 15 feet from my hole concealt in grass.

September 22: Kilt a Coyote and eat him all up.[15]

Shortly after the scouts were rescued, Shlesinger resigned from the command and returned to New York. He told his friends about his participation in the Beecher Island battle but no one believed him. When he produced some of his Indian battlefield relics, even a bloodstained blanket, his friends were still not convinced. In fact, one of his former friends asked, "How much did they cost?"[16] Two years later, Shlesinger moved to Cleveland where his stories of the battle continued to be met with disbelief. There was no evidence at hand to corroborate his story.

Shlesinger never received credit for being in the battle until August, 1893, some twenty-five years later, when General Fry's article appeared. It put an end for good to the doubts about Shlesinger's exploits, for the article contained these verses which immortalized the young scout:

"When the foe charged on the breastworks,
With madness and despair,
And the bravest souls were tested,
The little Jew was there.

When the weary dozed on duty
And the wounded needed care,
When another shot was called for,
The little Jew was there.

With the festering dead around them,
Shedding poison in the air,
When the crippled chieftan ordered,
The little Jew was there."[17]

In 1895, General Forsyth's version of the battle was published in *Harper's Magazine*. It contained the names of all the participants, further giving Shlesinger the recognition he deserved.

Two years later, Forsyth received a letter from Rabbi Henry Cohen of Galveston, Texas, in connection with Shlesinger. The general, then living in Wilkes Barre, Pennsylvania, replied:

My dear Rabbi Cohen:

In answer to your inquiry of December 7, regarding Mr. Sigmund Shlesinger, who served in my command on the Western frontier in 1867-68, and who was with me in my fight with the Sioux Indians in the Arickareee Fork, I have a high admiration of the courage and splendid pluck and endurance of young Shlesinger on the occasion mentioned...

He had never been in action prior to our fight with the Indians and throughout the whole engagement which was one of the hardest, if not the very hardest, ever fought on the Western plains, he behaved with great courage, cool persistence and a dogged determination that won my unstinted admiration as well as that of his comrades, many of whom had seen service throughout the War of Rebellion on one side or the other.

I can accord him no higher praise than that he was the equal in manly courage, steady and persistent devotion to duty and unswerving and tenacious pluck of any man in my command.

It is a real pleasure to state this fact. I especially mention the pluck and endurance of this young son of Israel and speak of him as a worthy descendant of King David.

> I am, sir, with sincere respect,
> Very truly yours,
> George A. Forsyth
> General, U. S. Army[18]

Over the years, Shlesinger corresponded with many of his old comrades. Some came to Cleveland to visit him, and he traveled around the country to visit them. The scouts had a spirit of comradeship that was quite touching, and, in fact, had formed the Beecher Island Battle Memorial Association to keep alive the memory of the little band of scouts who fought so nobly for their country.

Circa 1910, Shlesinger, then in his sixties, wrote the association at large, describing his friendship with Jack Stillwell.

> Jack and I were the only boys in the company and naturally gravitated toward each other. We were friends as soon as we met and chums before we knew each others' names. When Stillwell finally returned not long after the Carpenter rescue party arrived...Jack jumped from his horse and in his joy to see so many of us alive...permitted his tears free flow down his good honest cheeks. I kept up correspondence with him all these past years. Last year, he died. He was a big-hearted, jovial fellow, brave to a fault.

Shlesinger, in addition, wrote of his friendship with Jack Peate:

> One day a man came to my office asking for Sig Shlesinger, and introducing himself as J. J. Peate...You who have met Jack do not need to be told who and what Jack is. You know him to be the personification of all that is generous, kind and noble in a man, exceeded only by his better half. But to me, who had been hungering for a material manifestation of that cherished dream of long ago—to me, who had been longing to meet a comrade, face to face, he was almost an apparition. He was the first man connected with Forsyth's scouts to shake my hand in a grip of fellowship. It thrilled my whole being, and I am happy to be counted among his friends to this day, and I hope I always will be...

Continuing his letter to his comrades, Shlesinger wrote:

> Father time exacts his toll. Our years make us susceptible to the inevitable, and when the last one will have answered the eternal call, I would love to believe that kindred souls may resume that cohesive existence of which this world may be the prelude.

He closed his letter with this maxim:

I expect to pass through the world but once; if, therefore, there be any kindness that I can show or any good thing that I can do, let me do it now for I shall not pass this way again.[19]

Sigmund Shlesinger, one Jew among the Indians, or, more strictly, one Jew among 1,000 Indians, died in April, 1928. He was seventy-nine years old. The leaders of the Cleveland Jewish community came to his funeral to pay their respects to the man who worked tirelessly for so many Jewish causes. Rabbi Abba Hillel Silver, who conducted the services, paid tribute to Shlesinger, citing him for his leadership in philanthropic activities. The Board of Trustees of The Temple, in a resolution, saluted him as a fifty-year member "who labored in every cause."[20] His widow, Fannie, and his three children, mourned the loss of a good husband and father; and we can believe with utmost certainty—at least those of us can who have that turn of mind—that as the rabbi spoke, praising Shlesinger as a pillar of the community, the two older children, Lillian and Louis, scarcely heard a word the rabbi said. For they were thinking about that day, many years before, the day they had never forgotten, when Buffalo Bill came to town and they sat in a special box seat with their father and watched the battles between the cowboys and the Indians.

One mourner attended the funeral who was a stranger to the Jews of Cleveland, and clearly looked out of place among them. He was a bent, grizzled old man in his eighties who had traveled to Cleveland from Beverly, Kansas, to say farewell to a good friend and fallen comrade. He was alone now, this old man, the last surviving member of the little band of scouts who fought so bravely on the Arickaree Fork. His name was Jack Peate.[21]

Chapter 2

TROUBLE AT THE INDIAN OFFICE

For a brief period during Ulysses S. Grant's first term as president, the lives of two men who held important posts at the Bureau of Indian Affairs, one an Indian, the other a Jew, became closely intertwined in trying to establish peace during the most crucial period in white-Indian relations. In spite of their efforts, their work came to naught, thwarted in one case by intolerance and suspicion and in the other by accusations of fraud and mismanagement, both coming from strange and paradoxical adversaries.

The story begins on the day of President Grant's inauguration, January 20, 1869.[1] It was after the dark days of the Civil War, after the unsuccessful effort to remove Andrew Johnson from the presidency. The wounds of the war were beginning to heal, and hope had been restored to the people, their eyes now focused eagerly on the land west of the Mississippi, toward expansion and greater economic opportunity. In the West there were great new rivers to cross, dreams to come alive, hopes to fulfill, even though years before much of the land they coveted had been granted in perpetuity to the Indians.

No one expected the new president to deliver anything but a routine and hopeful inaugural address, and certainly not a controversial one. But that was not the case. With opinion divided over settlement of the West and how to deal with the

Indians, Grant, in a startling statement, told the nation that "the proper treatment of the original occupants of the land—the Indians—is one deserving of careful study. I will favor," he said, "any course toward them which tends to their civilization and ultimate citizenship."[2]

Grant's statement was astonishing. To civilize the marauding savages who were constantly doing battle with the white man was utterly out of the question. To make citizens of them? Impossible.

Grant was declaring that the Indians had the right to their land as well as the right to stand side by side in society with the white man.[3] If the nation had expected Grant to make any statement at all with respect to the Indian question, it would have been one in keeping with his military background, most likely a re-assertion of the hard-line positions of Generals William Tecumseh Sherman and Philip Sheridan, the spokesmen for all those who favored resolving the Indian problem through force. Sherman reasoned that, while the Indians had suffered many injustices at the hands of the government, western expansion was unstoppable, and any humanitarian gestures toward the Indians would be short-lived, for in the end their extermination was inevitable.[4] Sheridan's famous formulation was chilling. "The only good Indian," he said, "is a dead Indian."

Grant's statement came as good news to the reformers, the various Christian ministries and their followers, who were determined to save the Indians' souls and to make sure they were treated in a more humane way. Important to them as well was the need to clean house at the Bureau of Indian Affairs, the Indian Office, a corrupt agency of the Department of Interior. The church groups, in fact, in the months between Grant's nomination and his inauguration, lobbied strenuously to have politically appointed Indian agents replaced by missionaries.[5]

Grant had some more surprises in store for the nation. To oversee white-Indian relations, which were now strained to the breaking point, he appointed to the post of Commissioner of Indian Affairs, Brigadier General Ely Samuel Parker, his aide-de-camp during the Civil War and a longtime trusted friend. The appointment was a surprise because Parker, who was present with Grant at General Lee's surrender at Appomatox and had, in fact, helped draft the surrender documents, was a full blood Seneca Indian.[6] His new post as head man at the Indian Office meant that it would be up to an Indian to try to harmonize the contrary objectives of Indians and whites. Not only that, it meant that Parker, at the same time, would have to reconcile the equally disparate objectives of three other groups who sought to control the Indian Office: the politicians who had served as Indian agents before Grant took office, many of whom were flagrantly corrupt; the military who would like nothing better than to annihilate the Indians; and finally the church groups who sought to convert the Indians and, in so doing, civilize them.

As inconsistent as Parker's appointment was, almost as astonishing was Grant's selection of Dr. Herman Bendell, an Albany, New York, physician, as Superintendent of Indian Affairs for the Arizona Territory, the home of the especially belligerent Apaches. Bendell had served as a major in the Civil War later being breveted a Lieutenant Colonel, and like Parker was at Appomatox with Grant. His appointment was even more of a surprise than Parker's. First, Bendell was a Jew, and as a Jew he would find it hard to win the support of the Christian ministries whose overriding mission was to Christianize the Indians; and, second, he was appointed by the same "anti-semitic" Ulysses Grant who, in 1862, repeatedly criticized the activities of Jewish traders for selling cotton to the Confederacy and who finally in that same year had issued General Order 11, expelling all Jews from the Department of the Tennessee.[7]

White-Indian relations had been on a disastrous course ever since the end of the Civil War. The movement of white settlers to the West had gone forward relentlessly. Indians living in one place were driven to another, each new location providing less land than the previous one.[8] Farmers, ranchers, trappers and prospectors, carried west by the Iron Horse, swarmed across land which had once been given to the Indians "for as long as the grass shall grow"—land with unlimited access to water, land with plenty of grass for grazing, land rich in minerals and timber. In the process, treaties were broken, promises forgotten, for it would be unthinkable for an expanding nation to let heathen savages maintain possession of such valuable land. As a result treaties were negotiated in which the Indians agreed to cede their land to the government in return for annuities paid in the form of money, food and clothing. On the surface, the treaties seemed to be good for the Indian, but in numerous instances the Indians were swindled by crooked traders who grossly over-charged them for food, clothing and farm implements of inferior quality. All the while, corrupt Indian agents, using their agencies as a private money preserve, employed an array of schemes to defraud the Indians, usually in concert with the Indian traders.[9] There seemed to be no recourse for the Indians but to wage war against the government and the white settlers. With an Indian Office that was clearly in league with the white man, what other way was there for the Indians to redress their grievances?

In 1867, Senator James R. Doolittle of Wisconsin spearheaded the establishment of a peace commission. Its goal was to study the settlement of the West, but more specifically the commission wanted to look at ways to accommodate the Indians who would have to step aside to make room for white settlements. The commission was chaired by then Commissioner of Indian Affairs, Nathaniel G. Taylor. The members included four civilians, one of whom was Taylor, and four army generals, Sherman being the most forceful and best known of the generals. Sherman continued to argue that the westward thrust of the white man was as inevitable as the Indian's ultimate extermination. The recommendations of the commission, however, were in sharp contrast with Sherman's arguments and became the basis for Grant's inaugural day proclamation calling for the Indian's civilization and citizenship. There was a nobility about Sherman. Ethical and realistic, Sherman deplored the corruption that was taking place in the Indian Office, and had gone along with the commission's recommendations only because they called for the replacement of dishonest Indian agents.[10]

The commission's findings were released in January, 1868. Said Taylor at the time, "Nobody pays any attention to Indian matters. This is a deplorable fact. Members of Congress understand the negro question and talk learnedly of finance and other problems of political economy but when the progress of settlements reaches the Indian's home, the only question is 'how best to get his lands.'"[11]

As part of the work of the peace commission, treaties were signed in 1868 with the Indians who agreed to stay on their reservations and accept the efforts of the government to civilize them. Grant, then commanding general of the army, ordered Sherman to destroy three army bases in the west.[12]

Before Grant's inauguration. Parker and Grant began drafting a peace plan, Grant's peace program, as it came to be known. Its objectives were to end a treaty system that pre-supposed each tribe to be a sovereign nation; to treat the Indians as individuals responsible for their own welfare rather than as members of a tribe; to contain the Indians on reservations; and finally to educate them.[13] It was already understood that Grant's former aide de camp would be appointed commissioner. The two men set about planning the replacement of dishonest agents, the key recommendation of the peace commission. At first, their plan called for bringing only missionaries into the Indian service, in keeping with the ideas of the ministries and their wealthy and influential supporters. The representative societies of all the churches were then asked to recommend new agents, some reservations being assigned to Roman Catholics, some to Lutherans, some to Baptists, some to Presbyterians, and so on.[14] However, the plan which was put into effect just after Grant took office was later modified to include as agents a combination of missionaries and responsible army officers.[15] Grant was not a church-goer, but he trusted the missionaries, and he also trusted men like himself—military men who could be counted on to carry out their assignments as Indian agents just as they would any other assignment.[16]

The extermination of the Indians was then well on the road

to becoming a reality. The millions of Indians estimated to have been living in America when Columbus arrived had shrunk to about 250,000.[17] Among the surviving tribes were the powerful Sioux in the northern territory. In Wyoming and Colorado there were the Cheyennes, and farther south the Arapahos. There were also the Comanches of Texas, and the Apaches, Navajos and pueblo Indians of New Mexico and Arizona. The effects of disease, mass execution and assimilation had taken their toll, but equally devastating was the destruction of the Indian's spirit.[18] Westward expansion, interrupted by the Civil War, had started again. Once more, Indian land was being overrun by whites, and the Indians, in the fall of 1868, were again on the warpath. Grant's peace program, it seemed, had come at the right time.

In 1869, a month after Grant assumed the presidency, Congress passed legislation creating a Board of Indian Commissioners whose purpose was to serve as a watchdog over the Indian Office. Nine men were appointed to the board, including William Welch, a wealthy Philadelphian and Episcopalian, and Vincent Colyer, a self-appointed do-gooder and philanthropist who was a member of the Society of Friends as well as a member of the Christian Commission. There were no military men on the board, no Indians, no southerners, only wealthy religiously affiliated reformers. Even Parker, the new Commissioner of Indian Affairs, was not a member of the board, although, ironically, establishing a Board of Indian Commissioners had originally been Parker's idea. But it had developed into a far more powerful group than the bi-racial body Parker had envisioned.[19]

Members of the board never understood the Indian. The Indians' beliefs and attitudes, rooted in thousands of years of tradition, were a mystery to the reformers. Ignorant as they were of the deeper aspects of the Indian's heritage, they apparently made no effort to understand it or try to integrate Christianity into Indian culture. Instead, theirs was a single-minded campaign to mass-produce converts, and through Christianity, the reformers believed, Indians could enjoy a better life, their suffering alleviated.[20]

General Eli Parker served as Commissioner of Indian Affairs from January, 1869 until March, 1871. He was the embodiment of everything that a man of his race could accomplish, and Grant reasoned that what was true for his friend could be true for other Indians as well.[21] But acculturating the Indian was only a part of Grant's goal. Beyond that, Grant wanted to rid the Indian Office of the corrupt agents whose illicit activities were exacerbating the Indian problem. Moreover, his sympathy for, and a genuine desire to help, the Indians was reason enough to reject the exclusive use of military men as agents. That was why Grant had been agreeable to the entreaties of the wealthy and influential supporters of the various Christian denominations.

Apparently, Grant's appointment of Parker was not just symbolic; he was a friend who happened to be an Indian. But Bendell's appointment, on the other hand, had to be political. Grant had been convinced that having a Jew in the Indian Office would be appropriate. All of the faiths would then be represented, not just Catholic and Protestant. It is also possible that in appointing a Jew, Grant might have been eager to change the anti-semitic image that grew out of his issuance of the notorious General Order 11. Grant's biographer, William S. McFeely, offers a balanced view of Grant's behavior with regard to General Order 11. He points out that Grant was anti-semitic, but no more or less than most others of the period. There were entrepreneurs of all faiths who were profiteering in cotton, but Grant, before the Vicksburg campaign, had experienced a number of challenges to his authority, and, according to McFeely, may unconsciously have indulged in the age-old practice of displacing his personal frustrations onto the Jews.[22]

Herman Bendell was nominated December 7, 1870, and five weeks later was confirmed by the senate. He served as Superintendent of Indian Affairs, Arizona Territory, from January 12, 1871 until spring, 1873.[23] There was some opposition to his appointment, ostensibly for reasons of protocol. Roscoe Conkling, a senator from New York opposed the appointment because he believed he should have had the privilege of appointments from his state. A congressional delegate from Arizona,

Richard C. McCormick, also opposed Bendell because he believed he should have been consulted first.[24] Nevertheless, Bendell received notice of his confirmation in mid-January together with a request to post a $50,000 surety bond. His annual compensation was set at $2,000,[25] $500 more than the agents who would be reporting to him. He was to succeed Colonel G.L. Andrews as superintendent and would be reporting from his post in Arizona City to Commissioner Eli Parker in Washington. At the time, Parker had been commissioner for nearly two years, and was already in heated conflict with the Board of Indian Commissioners.[26]

It's doubtful whether Bendell had any previous experience with Native Americans, and there is nothing to lead one to believe that at the time of his confirmation he had any strong feelings either way as to what kinds of agents should be assigned to the tribes, military or missionary. Prior to his appointment his range of experience was fairly narrow, centering primarily on his army service and on his medical training and practice in Albany.

The man responsible for Bendell's nomination was Simon Wolf, a Jew and a friend of Grant. Wolf was Recorder of Deeds for Washington, D.C. in 1869, the year that Grant created the Board of Indian Commissioners and authorized the Christian ministries to nominate trustworthy men to serve as agents and administrators at the Indian Office. Wolf was a self-appointed representative of American Jewry who had previously served as consul general to Egypt, and was concerned with protecting the rights of his co-religionists.[27]

Wolf, who was brought into frequent contact with political leaders through his own political and humanitarian activities, convinced Grant that a Jew should have a post at the Indian Office since other religious denominations were to be represented. Wolf also told Grant that a Jew would have no designs on the souls of the Indians as the Christians would have, and further would seek a better life for the Indians without any religious considerations.[28] Grant liked the idea, and asked Wolf to come up with a qualified Jewish candidate. Since none came to Wolf's mind, he approached his friend, Simon W. Rosendale, a well known political figure who had been Attorney General of New York state. Rosendale recommended Bendell, his boyhood friend and B'nai B'rith colleague.[29]

In taking note of Bendell's nomination, the editor of *The Voice of Israel* wrote:

> The trouble with the Red Men has perhaps been occasioned by pious evangelical commissioners who worked to save their souls and let their benighted bodies take care of themselves. An honest agent [sic] of the Jewish faith will attend to the strict letter of his official duties, and will not allow "the poor Indian" to be forced unwillingly into any religious conversion.[30]

To the notion expressed in some newspapers that the Indians would be better served by a non-Jewish superintendent who would work to the conversion of the Indians, *The Voice of Israel,* in a later editorial, expressed the hope that the teachings of the B'nai B'rith—"benevolence, brotherly love and harmony"—would be implanted "in the breast of every Indian in the territory, and convince them that these are the faith and practice of every good man, be he Jew or Gentile."[31]

Bendell was born in Albany, October 28, 1843, the son of Edward Bendell, a Jewish immigrant from Germany who made his living in Albany as a *schochet*, a butcher.[32] In 1861, when he was eighteen, Bendell left his studies at Albany Medical College and enlisted as a hospital steward in the Garibaldi Guard, a regiment of foreign born residents of New York City. A year later he resigned from the army to complete his medical studies in Albany, and in 1863 rejoined the army as assistant surgeon in the Sixth New York Heavy Artillery, later serving as surgeon in the 86th New York Volunteers.[33] At the time he was confirmed for his post at the Indian Office, he was twenty-eight and unmarried.

Eli Parker was born on the Tonawanda reservation in New York in 1828.[34] A Seneca chief, he was the grandson of the famous orator and *sachem*, Red Jacket. He was also known as Ho-Se-No-An-Da. Eli's father, William Parker, also a Seneca chief, had fought the British in the war of 1812, and took the name Parker from a British captive who had lived with the Parker family.[35]

Parker had been an excellent student at Mission schools and at Yates and Cayuga academies. He read law for three years but was denied admittance to the bar because, like most Indians, he was not a citizen. This denial of his ambition did not deter him from pursuing a career as a professional. He next enrolled as a student of engineering at Rensselaer Poytechnic Institute, and after graduation became an engineering supervisor on a number of federal construction projects—lighthouses, canals, hospitals and customhouses.[36]

While on assignment in Galena, Illinois, Parker, in the late 1850s, met Ulysses Grant who was then working as a clerk at a leather store. It was in Galena that the two men became acquainted.[37] At the outbreak of the war, Parker returned to New York state and tried to enlist in the army as an officer. He contacted Secretary of State William Henry Steward for a commission, but Steward, who also hailed from New York state, was of no help, reportedly having told Parker that the war "was an affair between white men and one in which the Indian was not called to act." Parker, however, continued to pursue his dream of getting an army commission, and finally connected, becoming a captain on Grant's staff during the Vicksburg campaign. He served on Grant's staff until the end of the war, and went along to Grant's headquarters in Washington after the war. The two men were fond of each other, and Grant was happy to have around him this tall, hulking Indian with his polished white man's ways.[38]

Parker earned advancement to the brevet rank of Brigadier General, eventually winning citizenship because of his war record. For technical reasons, he was denied the right to vote, but for an Indian living at a time when feelings ran high against his people, Parker was remarkably well accepted, highly regarded by white intellectuals in Washington and frequently sought after by politicians and military men. There did not seem to be any barriers to his complete assimilation into white society, and he became a joiner of clubs and fraternal organizations. It is easy to understand why he came to believe that since he could bring down the racial barriers, other Indians had the potential to do the same.[39]

From its very beginning, the Indian Office has had a commissioner as its head, and Parker was the first and only Indian ever to occupy that seat. The need for an Indian Office had never been more important than during the settlement of the West. There were two great conflicting forces—on the one hand the white man seeking access to Indian lands and represented in that quest by Congress through the Department of the Interior, and on the other hand the Indian, determined to protect his lands. Until the Indian Office stepped into the breech, it had been a battle staged without a referee.[40] Deplorable as was the plight of the Indians, it would have been far worse if there had been no Indian Office, and no matter how corrupt and mismanaged it was, the Indian Office was the only agency that stood between the Indian and his "utter annihilation and degradation."[41]

The people on the firing line in the Indian Office were the Indian agents, men who worked within the reservations as combination reservation managers, purchasing agents and go-betweens for all those who wanted to have dealings with the Indians. They were the direct link of the government with the Indian,[42] but because of the wholesale corruption of so many of the agents something had to be done, and Grant, all too simplistically perhaps, thought that using missionaries as agents was the way to repair this most vital connection.

When Bendell reported for duty in Arizona in March, 1871, he was quickly initiated into territorial problems. As soon as he arrived he was confronted with the news that marauding Apaches were wantonly murdering white settlers in a new outcropping of violence. Such forays had been a persistent problem in Arizona for several years, and *The Arizona Miner* took note of it by printing a list of whites murdered by Indians in the years between 1864 and 1871. In effect, the newspaper called for a declaration of war against the Apaches, and sought public support to "overthrow and subdue the red miscreants...who will eventually make one desperate effort to kill us or drive us from the territory if earnest and vigorous war is not speedily made upon them...(to) speedily sweep the last savage murderer now in existence into eternity."[43]

It was a difficult time for a new man to arrive on the scene. A month after he arrived, Bendell was informed that on April 29, 1871, a party of white citizens of Tucson, accompanied by Mexicans and Papago Indians, had gone on an Apache hunt and within two days had slain eight-five of the tribe and had captured twenty-eight others in what has come to be known as the Camp Grant massacre. Bendell sent Parker an impartial report of the affair, noting that ammunition and personal belongings of whites murdered by Apaches at an earlier time had turned up at the site. *The Arizona Miner* applauded the massacre. "Farewell, defunct Pinals (Pinal Apaches)," it wrote, "you have met a just fate; you are good Indians now."[44]

A few weeks before the massacre, Bendell had written in his first status report to Parker: "I arrived at the Superintendency in March of 1871," wrote Bendell, "and on the 13th received from my predecessor, Colonel George L. Andrews, the office property pertaining to the department." He went on to inform Parker that he had established communications with special agents at the Colorado and Gila reservations; that a group of Pima Indians had been guilty of several depredations; and that he himself intended to visit reservations to get familiar with conditions and thereby be able "to determine what might be desirable to recommend to the Department hereafter."[45]

Pleading the Indian's case, Bendell told Parker: "I feel it is a duty I owe to the people of the Country and the Indians under my charge to do something to relieve the pressures that surround them, and earnestly solicit the Department to accord to me a discretionary power in the matter, or furnish me with such instructions as may be operated (upon) immediately."[46]

In subsequent reports, Bendell demonstrated compassion for the Indians but deplored the idea of treating them permissively, this in keeping with the tenets of Grant's peace program. It was evident that Bendell's aim was to foster the Indian's independence and self-reliance, even though they were wards of the government. In that regard, he had a number of recommendations. He called for the establishment of industrial schools on the reservations; he asked for more intelligent management in the distribution of water, noting that irrigation for agricultural activities makes more sense than providing the Indians with stipends, for he believed that giving them annuities was a plague. "They are naturally lazy and worthless, as seen from our standpoint," he conceded, and cautioned that anything which adds to that condition only makes matters worse. He called for interpreters to educate the Indians and to teach them habits of cleanliness, and asked for proper hospital facilities to treat the sick, many of whom were infected with syphilis. Finally, he asked the government to ask the missionary societies to divert funds from their work with the "heathen abroad to the heathen here."[47]

Bendell's efforts to improve the lives of the Indians did not mitigate his tough stance in maintaining discipline. In fact, the militantly anti-Indian *Arizona Miner* paid tribute to Bendell when he left the superintendency in 1873:

> Dr. H. Bendell, ex-Superintendent of Indian Affairs for the Territory, is now on his way to Washington, having been relieved by Dr. Tanner (J.A. Tanner). During Dr. Bendell's long stay here, his intercourse with our people was pleasant and agreeable, and, having had the honor and manliness to take the right course on the Indian question, upon almost every occasion, he was not liked by General Howard (O.O. Howard) nor by V. Colyer, but for having done so, his memory will live in the hearts of many of our people, and, in their name, we wish him a pleasant journey and a full share of life's blessings.[48]

Neither Parker nor Bendell was any more or less dedicated than the other toward solving the Indian problem. Both men wanted to transform the Indians into settled, self-supporting farmers and ranchers. But their approaches differed on one important matter. Parker believed that the belligerency of the

Indians could be defused by offering adequate subsistence on a regular basis through designated Indian agents, and that the reservation tribes could be disciplined if they got out of hand through the withholding of subsistence. He did not appear to share Bendell's view that subsistence would weaken their will and drain their initiative. In keeping with Parker's attitude, he emphasized the need to imbue the Indians with Anglo American tastes and values. Their acculturation, in Parker's mind, was consistent with the "civilization and "citizenship" of Grant's inauguration address, the very foundation of the president's peace program.[49]

Parker was stern and paternalistic in dealing with his charges, exactly like the white Washington officials he was acquainted with. He himself had been determined to become assimilated into the world of the white man, and he had succeeded—so much so that his critics dubbed him "the white man's Indian." His white friends had given him credit for having become a general in the army, but later in life when he was given a succession of only minor jobs he came to realize that no matter how much he had tried to adapt to the white man's world, no matter how many clubs and fraternal organizations he had joined, he was still an Indian.[50]

In Parker's scheme of things, the Indians who stayed on the reservation and behaved themselves were "friendly" Indians and were to be rewarded with stipends, while those who strayed off the reservation were "unfriendly," their stipends to be withdrawn. He preached to his fellow Indians that there was more to lose by resisting change than by accepting it, and he was prepared to take military action against the tribes when all of his monetary enticements had failed.[51]

Parker's downfall was brought about by the Board of Indian Commissioners and by its chairman, William Welch, who was dedicated to helping the Indians through Episcopalian Indian missions. In Welch's eyes the Indians were fascinating people, and he was captivated by their "seductively different ways" and by the "splendid challenge their culture afforded those who would have the joy of cleansing it with Christianity."[52]

Welch, enormously wealthy and powerful, fancied himself as the spokesman for the Indian cause, and as chairman of the Board of Indian Commissioners was irritated at the way Parker was running the Indian Office. He became angry if Parker did not consult with him, and accused Parker of being unqualified for his job. The two men feuded continuously, and perhaps at the core of the disagreements was Welch's persistent demands that certain tribes be transferred from Quaker agents to Episcopalian agents. The feuding became so intense that Welch resigned from the board, and thereafter became a gadfly, waging his own private battle against Parker.[53]

From the first, Parker secretly had some misgivings about the church-state alliance in oversight of the Indians, even as did Grant, and was fearful of the chaos that might arise when a host of rival Christian sect representatives, each trying to drive his own claim-stake into the soul of the Indian, were brought in as agents. With Welch's self-interested hawking of the Episcopalian cause, Parker's fears were well founded.[54]

After his resignation, Welch continued to monitor the affairs of the Indian Office, somehow being able to scrutinize all the administrative activities of the office. Finally, in December, 1870, at the time Bendell was nominated for his superintendency, Welch sent letters to the Department of the Interior accusing Parker of fraud and wastefulness. In all, there were thirteen different categories of charges, including allegations that Parker illegally signed private documents for large quantities of food, that he violated laws in soliciting from traders bids for provisions, that he used shoddy accounting practices, that he wasted funds on unnecessary materials and on inflated freight charges, that he made improper tribal allocations, that he retained employees for political reasons, and on and on. The charges were investigated by a sub-group of the House committee on appropriations, and during the inquiry Welch was permitted to examine witnesses and pore over Indian Office documents, becoming in effect both the accuser and the prosecutor.[55]

The investigating committee found "no evidence of any pecuniary or personal advantage sought or derived by the

Commissioner," and acquitted Parker of Welch's most serious accusations. Parker, however, acknowledged that he may have made some mistakes in handling various contractual details, and attributed them to his inexperience in these matters. Influential figures came to Parker's defense, characterizing him as a man of integrity. One such was Jacob Cox, former Secretary of the Interior. Even some members of the Indian commission came forward to plead Parker's case.[56]

The report of the hearings, released in February, 1871, cited several examples of irregularities in Parker's management of the Indian Office, "arising," it said, "partly from a vicious system inherited from the past, and partly from errors of judgement."[57] Even though he was cleared of willful misconduct, Parker's reputation was damaged, and he sent a letter of resignation to Grant. The president commended his old friend and aide de camp, wished him well, but accepted his resignation.[58]

Bendell also felt the intolerance of the ministries. Even from the beginning, he was opposed by the *Boston Pilot*, which found his appointment inappropriate. The Indians in Arizona and New Mexico were all Catholics, the *Pilot* wrote, and with the exception of the Apaches, the Arizona tribes are "well advanced in civilization," having long ago been converted to Christianity by Jesuit and Franciscan missionaries. *The Pilot* was fearful that Bendell would try to convert his charges to Judaism, and wrote that there was no need for the "missionary labor of an Israelite superintendent for these Indians, clothed with the authority to undo the work of the early Christian missionaries."[59]

The Jewish Times answered *The Pilot* by pointing out that if Grant's purpose in appointing Bendell was to give the Jews "an opportunity to propagate their faith amongst the Indians, he would have consulted the Jewish community as to the proper man to carry out their missionary duty." *The Times* further contended that Bendell would not have consented to go to Arizona as a Jewish missionary, "nor would he have likely been designated as such by the Jewish community if a religious mission were to be fulfilled by him." The *Times* editor also noted that Grant appointed Bendell merely "to signify his sense of equity by recognizing the Jewish church [sic], and according it the same privileges as the other denominations."[60]

It is puzzling, however, that *The Jewish Times* failed to take note of the fact that Judaism is not a proselytizing religion nor that, even if it were, Bendell was not a rabbi and thus not empowered to make conversions.

It is not known to what extent Bendell, during his more than two years as superintendent, felt the day to day pressure of being a Jew. However it may not have been his only problem. Undoubtedly, in addition to his being a Jew, his firmness in dealing with the tribes did not endear him to the powerful ministries who were well connected with the Indian Office and overly-permissive in their attitude toward the Indians. In June, 1873, Bendell resigned as superintendent, the resignation coming as a result of an event reported by Simon Wolf, the man who had spearheaded Bendell's appointment. As Wolf reports it:

> There was a board of missions connected with this Indian business with which General O.O. Howard and Mr. William Welch of Philadelphia, and other good Christian fellows were connected. Their purpose in meeting was to review the work of various superintendents...in behalf of the Indians. The report of the board as it pertained to Bendell: ...'a most excellent official...man of splendid judgement, strict integrity who has managed the affairs of the office to entire satisfaction, but unfortunately he is not a Christian.'[61]

In reporting the incident, Wolf noted that "it was such a startling and yet natural proposition emanating from this source that for a moment I did not reply." He added that he then gave the board a lecture about American citizenship "but it proved ineffectual, the missionary element, dominant and assertive, won the day."[62]

Bendell returned to Albany in the fall of 1873 and married his longtime sweetheart, Wilhelmine Lewi. Shortly afterwards, he served for a year as U.S. Consul to Denmark, then settled down in Albany to practice ophthalmology and otology. In 1893, he became president of the medical society of the State of New York. He died at the age of eighty nine in 1932, his wife Wilhelmine and three children surviving him.[63]

Eli Samuel Parker never recovered from Welch's efforts to discredit him. After he resigned as commissioner, he held a number of low-paying, minor jobs with the New York police department. No matter how far he had advanced in his lifetime, socially and professionally, he was, in the end, still regarded, in William Welch's words, as a man "but a remove from barbarism."[64]

Parker died in 1895, an obscure figure. As Henry G. Waltman points out in "Ely Samuel Parker," he probably "never suspected that a later generation of Native Americans might question his loyalties, methods, and goals. His ground-breaking executive activities in an age when the Indian's very existence was in jeopardy entitled him to more credit and recognition than posterity has given him."[65]

Greed, jealousy and intolerance are on-going evils that most likely will never disappear in spite of the good that some men try to do. Sooner or later each man's capacity to effect change will be exhausted, but, let us hope, men will continue to make the effort, as Parker, Bendell and Grant did. Vague as it may be, that is perhaps the only meaning one can derive from this unhappy tale, and these unfortunate incidents will underscore this sad truth:

Grant's peace program was a failure. The bloodiest battles with the Indians—200 in all—occurred during two decades, beginning with Grant's accession to the White House in 1869 and ending on a cold winter day in 1890 at Wounded Creek Knee in South Dakota. It was there that a ragtag band of 350 Sioux, 230 of them women and children, were annihilated, having been provoked into battle by a force of 500 soldiers. At Wounded Creek Knee on that bitter December day, there were no clergymen present after the slaughter, neither priest nor minister, to send the souls of the dead into the kingdom of God, or to bid their bodies farewell, as the young and old together were herded into a common grave.

By the middle of the 1880s, with only a quarter of a million Indians living on 187 reservations, the Bureau of Indian Affairs had grown into a bureaucracy of 2,500 employees, one employee for every 100 Indians.[66] At the time, a congressman observed that "no branch of the national government is so tainted with corruption, so utterly unworthy of a free and enlighted government, as the Indian Bureau."

At the San Carlos reservation in Arizona, government inspectors at the time had found the Indian agent "selling goods on the open market, diverting Indian cattle to his private herd, feeding the cattle government grain, and herding them with a government employee."[67]

In 1973, more than a hundred years after the missionaries took over as Indian agents, the influence of a pietistic Board of Indian Commissioners was still evident. According to *The Arizona Daily Star,* there were more than fifteen churches on the poor San Carlos reservation, "each dispensing its own distinct brand of Christianity." In the process, some Apaches believe, the missionaries "brought only confusion, not a better way of life." The missionaries "came in and approached us in the wrong way," said one Apache. "They didn't study the Apache religion. If they had, they would have realized that the Apaches were worshipping God. It's just that the Apaches weren't using the same tools or instruments such as the cross and the bible, as the white man." Some Apaches believe that Christianity has ruined the Apache culture, one Indian pointing out that "when Christianity came, the Apaches heard that everything they did was regarded as a sin."[68]

On January 12, 1991, nearly 160 years after the Bureau of Indian Affairs was established, the following news story appeared in *The New York Times:*

> WASHINGTON, January 11—A Federal investigation has found that the Bureau of Indian Affairs, which manages health, education and cultural programs on the nation's

Indian reservations, cannot account for $95 million appropriated to the bureau in the fiscal year that ended Sept. 30. That money amounts to nearly 10 percent of the agency's $1 billion annual budget. "It's been a fact for years that there are problems with that agency," said A. Gay Kingman, executive director of the National Congress of American Indians.

Chapter 3

UNCLE JULIUS'S LAST WALK

On a spring morning in 1909, a dapper sixty year old bachelor, the general agent in Omaha for the Provident Life Assurance Society, left his comfortable apartment over Adler's store, "The Fair," at Twelfth and Farnam street, and strolled down Farnam until he reached his brother Moritz's cigar store. He stopped and chatted with his brother, bought a cigar, lighted it, and said, contentedly, "Well, I think I will walk up the street a while and get some fresh air."[1]

He was in good spirits. For several weeks he had been recovering from ptomaine poisoning,[2] and was now almost completely well. As a resident of Omaha for over forty years, he had seen the city grow from a population of a few thousand to over 70,000. He had seen the city develop into an important railroad terminus with the completion of the Union Pacific Railroad and the entrance of the Rock Island, the Burlington and the Northwestern. And with the city's rise as a major railroad center, he had seen the growth of the meat packing industry in South Omaha.

He walked out of his brother's store with the assured air of a man who had made his mark. He had risen from poor immigrant German Jew to a beloved, affluent figure in what was fast becoming an important American city. Where once there were frame shacks along Farnam street, imposing multi-story buildings had now sprung up. Omaha was prospering, and he himself had contributed to that prosperity.

After walking a few steps up Farnam, he paused, turned, and waved to his brother. It was 10:30 AM, May 10, 1909. He then continued his walk—the last walk he would ever take.

An hour and a half later, a few minutes before noon, his body was found lying beside a bench in Hanscom Park, two miles from his brother's store. Two bullets had pierced his body, a revolver was clutched in his left hand.[3] His death was ruled a suicide, and it was claimed he had been despondent because of ill-health.

The man who died in Hanscom Park was outgoing and well-liked—one of Omaha's most spirited citizens. He had organized the Standard Club, the first social club of any distinction in Omaha. He had been one of the founders of Temple Beth Israel, and an active member of the local Hebrew Benevolent Society. He was a music lover, an accomplished musician who played the flute and violin, and he had organized a 117-piece orchestra, known as the Omaha Musicians Union, an orchestra which he himself had conducted at various times. As Omaha's foremost patron of the arts and a well-known party giver, he frequently played host to some of Europe's celebrated singers and musicians.[4]

His name was Julius Meyer. To his nieces and nephews and to many of the children of Omaha, he was Uncle Julius. But some forty years earlier, during a period of his life which he had now moved beyond, he was known as "Box-Ka-Re-Sha-Hash-Ta-Ka," a name bestowed upon him by the Pawnees who had adopted him into their tribe. It meant: "Curly-headed white chief who speaks with one tongue."

Julius Meyer was a man of accomplishments. Primarily an Indian trader, he operated the "Indian Wigwam," an Indian trading post on Farnam Street, from the late 1860's until the closing years of the nineteenth century. As a lad of sixteen, during the early days of his trading, Meyer served General George Crook, then commanding the Department of the Platte,[5] as an interpreter,[6] for in only a short time he had learned to speak six Indian tongues—Ponca, Brule Sioux, Omaha,

Winnebago, Pawnee and Oglala Sioux.[7] Standing Bear, Red Cloud, Sitting Bull and other chiefs were his friends.

In addition, he was a promotion man of talent, a master merchandiser of the Indian to white society. America and Europe were fascinated by the Indian—his customs, clothing and artifacts, and Julius made good mercantile use of that fascination.

The circumstances surrounding his death had the ingredients of an Agatha Christie story—mysterious, unsettling, ambiguous. To some, the circumstances continue to raise questions that will forever focus attention on a man who, while he lived, thrived on attention.

The saga of Julius Meyer is rooted in the early years of Jewish migration to the West. The first of these immigrants came to the Nebraska Territory in the early 1860's, attracted by the population boom in connection with the construction of the Union Pacific. Most had come from Germany, Austria and Hungary. and settled in Omaha. While many remained in Omaha, others followed the railroad's construction route west, eventually settling in Grand Island, Fremont, Columbus and North Platte.[8]

Omaha's population in 1860 was 1,880, but within ten years had soared to 16,000. Between 1863 and 1865, as the population began expanding, three brothers, immigrants from Blomberg, Germany, arrived in Omaha. They were Max, Moritz and Adolph Meyer. The youngest brother, Julius, arrived a few years later, in 1866, the year before Omaha was chartered as a city and Nebraska was proclaimed a state.[9]

The Meyer brothers, led by Max, the eldest, wasted no time getting into business. Each day new faces appeared on Farnam street. There were goods to sell, and no shortage of buyers.

Max's first business venture, which he operated with Moritz, was Max Meyer & Bro. Co., founded in 1866 as a cigar store. It was located on Farnam near Eleventh street. Adolph, in the meantime, started a jewelry and music business on Twelfth and Douglas. Three years later, in 1869, the two businesses merged and moved into a building at the northwest corner of Eleventh and Farnam.[10]

Julius, who was born in Blomberg in 1851, came to the U.S. in 1864 at age thirteen. A little over a year later, he arrived in Omaha, then a small, dusty settlement on the edge of the prairie, and almost at once began trading with the Indians. He would trade trinkets from Max's jewelry store and cigars made by his brother, Moritz, in return for Indian artifacts.[11] It was while engaging in his trading activities that he learned the language of the Indians.

Julius's "Indian Wigwam" was probably just another retail arm of Max Meyer & Bro. Co. Julius called himself a dealer in "Indian, Chinese and Japanese Curiosities,"[12] so it is logical to think that the oriental curiosities had been obtained through Max's supply sources. Evidently they were designed to increase traffic at the trading post, with little regard for their being consistent with its Indian image. The Indian curiosities, of course, were obtained by Julius himself from his Indian pals, and included beads, mocassins, wampum pouches, tomahawks, bows and arrows, petrifications, scalps, peace pipes and Indian dressed furs and skins. With an ever increasing number of people travelling to Omaha and beyond, the "Indian Wigwam" had rapidly become an important tourist attraction.

On his sojourns into Indian country, Julius, travelling on foot or horseback, would often live for weeks with the Indians, bedding down in their teepees and wigwams.[13] His mastery of the Indian language unquestionably endeared him to his Indian cronies, for few white men had ever made the same effort. Another factor accounting for Julius's success as a trader was the importance he seemed to place on dealing squarely with the Indians. Evidence of his integrity was the fact that the Indians had named him, "Box-Ka-Re-Sha-Hash-Ta-Ka."

Julius's relations with the Indians were social as well as commercial. Often he would be invited to Indian dog feasts, where the *piece de'resistance* was the boiled carcasses of dogs.

Sigmund Shlesinger, hero of the Battle of Beecher Island.
American Jewish Archives

Artist R.F. Zogbaum's depiction of Sigmund Shlesinger and
Colonel George Forsyth at the Battle of Beecher Island, 1868.
American Jewish Archives

Solomon Carvalho, *Self-Portrait*. Barbados, 1844.

John Charles Fremont. Portrait by Solomon Carvalho c. 1856.
Pennsylvania Academy of the Fine Arts, Philadelphia

Artist Byron E. Wolfe's depiction of the charge of Chief Roman Nose
at the Battle of Beecher Island, 1868.

American Jewish Archives

FRIDAY, SEPTEMBER 18, 1868.

in the night I dug my hole
deeper cut of meat off of
the Horses & hung it up on
Bushes, Indians made a Shore
on us at Day break, but
retreated Kept Shooting nearly all day they Put up a
White Flag, left us
at 9 o clock in evening
Raind all night

SATURDAY 19

the Indians came
back again Kept
sharpshooting all
day 2 Boys Started
for Fort Wallace
Raind all night

SUNDAY 20

Dr Moore died last
night Raining
part of the Day
snow about 2
inches thick
Indians Kept sharp
shooting

MONDAY, SEPTEMBER 21, 1868.

Scalpt 3 Indians
which where found
about 15 Feet from
my hole conseald
in Izaey

TUESDAY 22

Killt a Coyote & eat
him all up

WEDNESDAY 23

A page from the battlefield diary of Sigmund Shlesinger.

American Jewish Archives

Julius Meyer with Chief Standing Bear.
American Jewish Archives

Julius Meyer store, Omaha.
Nebraska State Historical Society

Julius Meyer with Indian Chiefs. (Standing): Meyer, Red Cloud;
(Seated): Sitting Bull, Swift Bear, Spotted Tail, ca. 1869
Nebraska State Historical Society

"Sken-What-Ux," (Elizabeth Friedlander), a descendant
of Colville chiefs and wife of a Jewish trader.
American Jewish Archives

Joseph Sondheimer, Muskogee, Oklahoma.
Oklahoma Historical Society Archives

Samuel Checote, principal chief of the Creek nation, 1869-1882.
Oklahoma Historical Society

Portrait of Walkara, the Ute chief, by the Jewish artist,
Solomon Carvalho. Original sketch by the artist was drawn during
the peace pow-wow ending the Mormon-Indian war, 1854.
The Thomas Gilcrease Institute of American History and Art

These feasts were special occasions, and it was an honor for a white man to be asked to attend. However, as a man who observed the Jewish dietary laws, Julius could not partake of the dog meat. Undaunted, the Indians served Julius hard-boiled eggs, for they knew from experience with other traders that Jews had no dietary problem eating eggs.[14]

Julius had the instincts of a showman at an early age, and the story is told that he once took along on one of his trading missions a show-business friend, a magician known as Herman the Great. Herman performed for the Indians, dazzling them with magic feats. One trick in particular had the Indians gaping in astonishment. It was when Herman extracted gold pieces with great flourish, seemingly out of his empty hat. That night, two Indians crept into the teepee where Julius and Herman slept, intending to scalp the magician in order to get their hands on Herman's magic hat. Fortunately, Julius awakened in time to thwart the assault.[15]

Julius's trading sojourns were never entirely without danger. On one trip he was confronted by a party of unfriendly Indians who had seized his pack and were ready to scalp him. Pawnee Chief Standing Bear came upon the scene and interceded in Julius's behalf, saving his life. That incident was the beginning of a friendship between the two that would last the rest of their lives.[16]

Julius's niece, Lena Rehfeld, later recalled that her uncle carried a scar on his forehead as a reminder of that episode. As for Standing Bear, "Uncle Julius never forgot him for that, and Standing Bear never wanted for anything while he lived that Uncle Julius could provide for him."[17]

Julius exploited his friendship with the Indians for commercial gain. Newspaper advertisements for the "Indian Wigwam" promoted Julius as an Indian trader and an Indian interpreter, and always noted his Indian name, "Box-Ka-Re-Sha-Hash-Ta-Ka." His promotion masterstroke, however, was in arranging for photographs with his Indian friends. In these photographs, Julius posed with such celebrated chiefs as Standing Bear; Red Cloud and Sitting Bull, both Oglala Sioux; and Swift Bear and

Spotted Tail, two Brule Sioux. In one photograph, Julius, bedecked in ornate Indian ceremonial garb, posed sitting before a campfire, peace pipe in hand, surrounded by six Indian warriors, each naked down to the waist.

Julius paid the Indians well for posing.[18] In another classic photograph, Julius, in his customary Indian dress, stands next to Red Cloud, while seated in front are Sitting Bull, Swift Bear and Spotted Tail. The photograph is said to have cost Julius the handsome sum of $800, for he had to bring the chiefs to Omaha and, in addition, give each of them two ponies for posing. This photograph, as well as others in which Julius posed with Indians, reveals a strange phenomenon of the nineteenth century—the Indians propensity for wearing white men's clothing and the white man's occasional inclination to wearing Indian attire. Julius's youthful Jewish face, sporting a black moustache from under an Indian headdress or coonskin cap, left little doubt which figure in the photos was Jewish and which was Indian.

The practice of cross-dressing between the two races was not an invention of Julius's but can be traced back to colonial times when the British presented the Indians with silver medals, gorgets and military coats.[19] Later, when Merriwether Lewis and William Clark confronted the Sioux chief, Weucha, in what is now South Dakota, they presented him with a military coat worn by the U.S. Artillery Corps. In 1839, a St. Louis doctor encountered a Sioux warrior wearing a red English uniform, and in the same year, William Ferris, a mountain man, ran across a large party of Teton Dakotas on the Platte. Several wore long scarlet coats trimmed with gold and silver lace.[20] Coats of this type later became known as "chief's coats."[21] The chief's coat, which is rarely seen today except in museums, was styled along military frock coat lines, and was regarded as a status symbol by the Indians. It was fashionable, expensive and, above all, it was worn by the white military whom the Indians grudgingly respected.[22]

In their photograph with Julius, Red Cloud, Swift Bear and Spotted Tail wear versions of the chief's coat, and for an additional touch of sartorial elegance, Swift Bear and Spotted Tail hold stove pipe hats in their hands. Ironically, it is only Julius and Sitting Bull who wear Indian dress (see photograph).

Julius wasn't the only white man with a penchant for dressing up in Indian clothing. The practice, however, was usually reserved for men who needed to establish their affinity with the Indians or who were showmen, or both. Merriwether Lewis posed for his portrait in authentic Nez Perce clothing. George Armstrong Custer posed in Indian dress in a photo taken at Fort Abraham Lincoln, and even went into battle on the Little Big Horn wearing a buckskin coat and fringed buckskin breeches. Lieutenant Stephen Mills, who commanded a company of Chiricahua scouts, wore Apache clothing to establish affinity with his troops. Both Dan Beard, one of the founders of the Boy Scouts, and Theodore Roosevelt, were photographed wearing Indian clothing.[23]

As a showman, Julius was well aware of the commercial value of establishing close ties with the Indians. By posing for photographs in Indian raiment, he sought to create the impression that he was an authentic frontiersman, a man deeply involved with the Indians and culturally inseparable from them. This was the same image that other celebrated showmen—Buffalo Bill, Deadeye Dick, Annie Oakley, Deadwood Dick and Buckskin Jack—tried to create by wearing Indian buckskin.

During the late nineteenth century, the white men in the East and in Europe were fascinated by the American Indian. Julius, who recognized an opportunity when he saw it, took a party of Indians to Europe for public appearances on one, perhaps two, occasions. The reports of the trips present a mixed picture. One source states that Julius took a group of Omahas and Winnebagos to the Paris Exposition of 1883, where they remained for three months.[24] But in an article in the *National Jewish Monthly*, Julius is said to have taken his Indian friends, Standing Bear included, to the Paris Exposition of 1889, the actual year of one of the expositions. (None was held in 1883). According to this source, the ocean trip was difficult, and the Indians got seasick during the voyage. Julius and his Indian companions reportedly remained in France for nearly a year.[25]

If Julius had travelled abroad in 1883, it would have historical significance. Carolyn Foreman, a noted Indian historian, wrote that "Indians were carried abroad for the purpose of exploiting them to enrich white men of the U.S," and noted, more significantly, that the idea originated in Omaha in 1883 but she does not name the originator.[26] Had a crossing been made in 1883, who else could have led it but Julius. For the next twenty-five years, Indians, in a continuous stream, crossed and re-crossed the Atlantic to entertain various heads of state. Buffalo Bill's "Wild West" Show, boasting a cast of seventy-five Sioux, made many crossings to perform in England, France, Austria, Spain, Hungary and Belgium—even the Vatican, but none of these crossings took place until 1887.[27] Another flamboyant showman, Gordon W. Lillie, known as Pawnee Bill, toured Europe with a troop of Indians, but not until 1894.[28]

Between 1866 and 1886, the Meyer brothers' business expanded rapidly, and after a series of moves settled at Sixteenth and Farnam in 1887.[29] Max and Adolph were partners in the jewelry and music operation while Max and Moritz formed the cigar partnership. Throughout this period, Julius ran his "Indian Wigwam,"[30] while at the same time maintaining a close business association with his brothers.

In its heyday at Sixteenth and Farnum, the Meyer firm, now doing business as Max Meyer & Bro. and Max Meyer & Co., was one of the largest retail outlets of its kind in the West. The cigar store had a twenty-five-foot frontage on Farnam and ran 132-feet in depth. Above the cigar store on the second floor, the brothers had located their wholesale jewelry and watchmaking operation. The third floor was used principally to store musical instruments.[31]

A shopper entering the store on Sixteenth street instead of on Farnam would come upon the jewelry and music store, crammed in great depth and breadth with jewelry, diamonds, watches, silverware, optical goods, musical merchandise, books and small instruments. The piano sales room, which was located on the second floor, was furnished with the elegance of a potentate's sitting room. The basement held back-up stocks of tobacco, together with a jewelry manufacturing operation. The firm had seventy-five employees, not including the twelve travelling salesmen who sold pianos, cigars and jewelry in Iowa, Nebraska, Colorado, Utah, Kansas, Wyoming and the Dakotas.[32]

Within a few years, however, the Meyer brothers' reign as mercantile kingpins came to an end. The big store at Sixteenth and Farnam, was destroyed by fire in 1889. The brothers tried to rebuild their business at another location, but it was too late. The business had passed its prime and eventually failed in the depression of 1893.[33]

Max, the leader of the Meyer clan, had been one of the most powerful men in Nebraska. He was an organizer of the Omaha Commercial Club, a forerunner of the Chamber of Commerce. He served four terms as president of the Omaha Board of Trade, and had been a charter member. He was, in addition, a principal of the Omaha Savings Bank, the first bank of its kind in Omaha.[34] Max left Omaha after the failure of the store and spent his remaining years in New York.

Adolph became an insurance salesman, and later moved to Chicago, pursuing the same occupation. He died suddenly in that city a short time later.

Moritz opened his cigar store, and Julius closed his "Indian Wigwam" forever. In all likelihood, Julius had been associated with Adolph in the insurance business until Adolph left for Chicago.

The news of Julius's death was a front page story in Omaha newspapers. In one account, the lead paragraph read:

> Lying beside a bench in Hanscom Park, a bullet hole in his left temple and another in his left breast, a revolver clenched in his left hand, the body of Julius Meyer, president of the Metropolitan Club and a resident of Omaha for over forty years, was found at 11:50 Monday forenoon...[35]

The article went on to point out that both his housekeeper and Mr. Adler, from whom he leased his rooms, could give no reason why he would have wanted to kill himself. Both asserted that Julius was in good spirits and well off financially.[36] His brother, Moritz, also was unable to explain the suicide. "He had been sick," Moritz was quoted as saying, "but was recovering. As far as I know, his financial condition was all right."[37]

The obituary went on to point out that "in making away with himself, he had evidently shot himself first in the temple and then turned the gun against his breast."[38]

On the one hand, Julius Meyer was a basic, practical-minded merchant, fearless enough to live among the Indians and trade with them. But there was another side to his character. He was also a butterfly in a prairie boom town—a man of culture, who loved music and enjoyed entertaining, and was fond of dressing up in Indian clothing. The true nature of his quest when he left Moritz's store on that spring morning in 1909 will remain forever buried in the past. Was he just another aging man, at peace with himself, out for a morning stroll, puffing on one of his brother's fine cigars? Or was some darkly destructive mission propelling him to Hanscom Park?

The people of Omaha could never explain the mystery of his death, and there is no record of any further investigation beyond the immediate ruling of suicide. In fact, the suicide ruling was rendered almost at the same time the body was discovered.

The puzzling fact, which was clearly apparent at the time, was how Julius could have shot himself in the temple without mortally wounding himself with that single shot. And if that shot had not killed him, why did he turn the gun against his breast instead of discharging the second bullet into his temple?

Julius's passion for posing for photographs with the Indians may provide an important clue to the mystery. In the photograph in which Julius is seen sitting around a campfire holding a peace pipe and surrounded by six Indian warriors (see photograph), Julius grips the peacepipe in his right hand. In still another photograph, Julius, wearing a coonskin cap and Indian buckskin breeches, has a knife and scabbard strapped to his right hip. These photos could conceivably indicate that Julius was right-handed. It does not seem likely that he would hold a gun in his left hand to do away with himself.[39]

Why would Julius, a happy, lifelong bachelor, stroll over to Hanscom Park, roughly a two-mile trip from his apartment on Farnam street to commit suicide when the deed could have been accomplished in his own apartment?

And if he had met with foul play, who would want to do away with that beloved little showman, "Box-Ka-Re-Sha-Hash-Ta-Ka"? And for what reason?

Julius's funeral services were private, held in the home of his sister, Mrs. Herman Rehfeld. A followup newspaper story noted that many letters and flowers were received at the Rehfeld home. All of the organizations of which Julius was a member—the musicians union, the Knights of Pythias, the Metropolitan Club and the Douglas County Pioneers, asked to attend the ceremony. The family said no because of the circumstances surrounding his death.[40]

Rabbi Frederick Cohn delivered a short eulogy,[41] then "Box-Ka-Re-Sha-Hash-Ta-Ka" was carted off to Pleasant Hill cemetery on his way to do some trading with the greatest Chief of them all.

Chapter 4

THE SHOT HEARD 'ROUND THE WEST

In a desolate part of Utah, six miles west of the little town of Deseret, on the north side of the Sevier River, stands a monument marking the site of the October 26, 1853 murder of Captain John Williams Gunnison of the U.S. Topographical Engineers and seven of his companions at the hands of the Pavant Indians.[1] The murder of Gunnison, whose remarkable surveying achievements paved the way for construction of the Union Pacific Railroad, changed the course of history in the West. To this day, his death remains a mystery and continues to plague the Mormon church and casts a shadow on the reputation of its prophet, Brigham Young.

The Gunnison monument can be viewed as more than just a reminder of an Indian massacre. It can symbolize much more—those brawling, turbulent times when the West was taking shape; when there were unlimited opportunities and precious few restraints; when all the forces that went into the formation of our nation were revealed—the lust, the passionately held religious beliefs, the staking out of new territory, the racial and religious clashes, and the never-ending struggle for power, the blind ambition and the unbridled greed. Disclosed out there in Utah Territory is the sad fact that the way men acted back in the 1850s, as we shall see, is still the way they act today.

The story begins on a warm September evening in Utah Territory, about a month before the murders actually took place.

A Pavant Indian brave, a member of a tribe thought to be peaceful, walks into a camp of newly arrived Mormons at Meadow Creek, near the town of Fillmore, where the large party of immigrants have stopped for the night. The Indian asks for food and gunpowder. The uneasy Mormons rudely turn away the Indian, and give no further thought to the incident.[2]

The Pavant tribe, through its chief, Kanosh, is friendly with the "Mormonees," the Mormons, and even with the "Mericats," non-Mormon whites, or gentiles. Kanosh's braves are accustomed to sounding out greetings to the occasional wagon trains that pass through the territory, for it gives them the chance to do some trading—moccasins and buckskin for those precious commodities of the white man, sugar and tobacco.[3]

The immigrant Mormons had been told earlier that a band of Pavants would also be encamped at Meadow Creek, near their own site, and had been told that they were friendly Indians and not to be afraid of them.[4]

Later that evening, the Pavant brave returns with eight more Pavants, armed with bows and arrows and a few rifles. Included in the party are Moshoquop, the tribe's war chief, and his elderly father, Tonif.[5]

The Indians beg for food, clothing and gunpowder. The settlers are apprehensive, the Indians saucy and belligerent.

Frightened at the sight of the Indians' weapons, the Mormons abruptly order the Indians to leave, but the Indians refuse, insisting that the land is theirs and announcing their intention to stay.[6]

A scuffle breaks out as the Mormons attempt to disarm the Indians. In the confusion, a shot is fired. Suddenly an Indian lies dead—not an ordinary brave but the old chieftain, Tonif, father of Moshoquop and an influential member of the tribe.

The shot that killed Tonif was the shot heard 'round the West. Its ultimate effect, the reprisal murder of Gunnison and his companions, was to reverberate eastward across the plains to the seat of government and thereafter down the corridors of time. Nothing in that part of the world would ever be the same.

The Mormon pioneers, forty in all, led by Thomas and John Hildreth, had come from Missouri. They had just left Salt Lake City with their cattle and sheep and were on their way to California. In the months just before their arrival, there had been several confrontations between the Mormons and the Ute Indians, an unfriendly tribe led by Chief Walkara. Some of the confrontations had led to killings on both sides in what had come to be known as Walkara's war, or sometimes as the Mormon-Indian War.[7]

The friendly Pavants were the favored tribe of Brigham Young, who then reigned over Utah Territory, not only as leader of the Mormons but also as territorial governor and Superintendent of Indian Affairs. When the Pavants had entered their camp, acting quarrelsome, the Mormon settlers in their panic had failed to make a distinction between the Pavants and the Utes.

A Mormon convert had joined the Hildreth party in Salt Lake City and would travel with the pioneers to California. He had come to Utah as a trader and was known variously as Levi Abrams, Levi Abraham and Abraham the Jew. His middle name should have been "trouble." It was most likely Abrams who fired the shot that killed Tonif.

Exactly which part of central Europe Abrams had come from can't be found in the Mormon annals. There is no record of how he arrived in the West, whether by the overland route or by the all-water or combined sea and land routes from the East Coast to San Francisco. Although there are questions about his origins, no doubts exist about his being a Jewish Mormon. He had been one of the first to abandon his ancient faith and follow the tenets of the Book of Mormon,[8] and his name appears on the Mormon rolls in 1853 and 1854.[9] He was one of the first Jews to settle in Utah, having arrived in 1853, perhaps earlier. He had converted to Mormonism in Fillmore around the time of his arrival in the territory.[10]

Abrams was a trader, like practically all the Jews who were

early settlers in the West. Around the time of the Gunnison massacre he had been embroiled in a court dispute with a freight hauler over merchandise owned by Abrams. Abrams had lost the case, and was fined $190.00.[11]

A Jew in Utah had a decided advantage in being a Mormon, a member of the Church of Jesus Christ of Latter-day Saints. Mormon tenets hold that their angel, "Mormon," was of Hebrew blood and that the Book of Mormon was originally written in the language of the Jews. Mormon literature repeatedly refers to their intention to restore the Jews to Palestine and to make Utah a second Zion. But when Young and his followers took Abrams into their fold—and he was only the third Jew to become a convert from the time the sect was founded in 1830—the Mormons suffered in the exchange, for Abrams was a trouble-maker, a man continually involved in disputes.

Abrams eventually stood trial for the murder of the old Pavant chieftain. The shot he fired that September night at Meadow Creek had set into motion a series of events that had a shattering impact on the Mormon church and on the federal government's administration of Utah Territory. For it was to result in the massacre by the Pavant Indians of Captain Gunnison and seven of his party—J. Creutzfeld, a botanist; the artist, R.H. Kern; William Potter; John Bellows; and army privates Liptrott, Caulfield and Merteens. The brutal killing of these men in turn was the crucial factor that weakened Young's power with the federal government, that ended his career as governor of Utah Territory, that destroyed his dream of an autonomous Mormon theocracy in the West, and finally that helped bring about the Utah invasion, the Mormon-Federal War of 1857-58.

Young and his followers, in their epic migration, removed themselves from Nauvoo, Illinois in 1847 and relocated in the Great Salt Lake basin in order to escape the strong anti-Mormon feelings of the gentiles.[12] Joseph Smith, the founder of the church, had been lynched in 1844, and the Mormons had previously been driven out of Ohio and Missouri. But here in Utah, they could worship freely and carry out their belief that a man could take several wives. From the time they arrived in Utah until 1853, when Gunnison and his companions were murdered, the Mormons, living now in a land where they were the only white men, had enjoyed a relatively peaceful existence, marred only by the hostile activities of the Ute Indians. The forty years following Gunnison's death, however, would be marked by violence and political upheaval.[13]

Two years after the Mormons arrived, Young organized the State of Deseret, the so-called "land of the honey bee," with Salt Lake City its capital. Young's dream was to have his own theocracy, a kingdom of God, with Young himself as head of the kingdom. But the dream was short-lived. The federal government, instead, created the territory of Utah, over Young's strenuous protests, and early in 1850, as a conciliatory gesture, President Millard C. Fillmore appointed Young to two posts: governor of the territory and Superintendent of Indian Affairs.[14] Utah Territory, occupying a vast expanse of western lands six times the size of the state of Pennsylvania, was situated between the Rocky Mountains and the Sierra Nevadas, from latitude 37 degrees to 42 degrees north.[15]

Young was a portly man, and of only medium height. But because of his commanding personality he could be a towering figure nonetheless. In his early fifties at the time, he was a brilliant and complex leader, power-hungry and lecherous, a man with nineteen wives and forty-nine children. His rule of Utah Territory was described as "a priestly tyranny."[16]

Young's weaknesses were his consuming hatred for the federal government and his overpowering and irrational need for complete autonomy, free from any interference from Washington. As his dream of his own State of Deseret slipped away, Young fell back on another tactic—to make Utah Territory a state. He reasoned that he would have far more autonomy as governor of a state than as a territorial stepchild, and to that end he repeatedly petitioned for statehood, petitions that would always be denied him.[17]

Even so, Young still ran the territory as if it were his own kingdom. He claimed infallibility with his followers, for his public instruction was always implied to have been given under divine inspiration. Any matters of government that were published in the official organ of the church, it was said, stood as "obligatory and binding in the highest possible degree."[18] There was no separation of powers—legislative, executive and judicial— and no freedom of elections. Candidates for state office who weren't Mormons could count on defeat. According to one observer, "the apostles in the church at Salt Lake are the legislators at Fillmore."[19]

When the Mormons arrived in Utah, there were about 12,000 Indians living in and around the Salt Lake basin—Gosiutes, Pavants, Shoshones, Navajos and Utes. These tribes had not been organized into nations but operated instead as independent renegade bands.[20] Resentful of the intrusion of the white man, the Indians stole the Mormons' livestock and attacked their settlements. But Young's attitude was permissive. He held that the Indians could be redeemed and could become a "pure and delightsome people."[21] He also thought he could bring about their acculturation and make Mormons of them. Joseph Smith had preached that the Indians "were a remnant of a scattered Israel, a fallen race whose ancestors' history was outlined in the Book of Mormon."[22] Thus, on the Mormons' part, there was a divine obligation to teach the Indians the ways of civilization and "the spiritual truth of the restored gospel."

Young had a four-point philosophy with respect to the Indians—treat them kindly but not as equals; punish them severely when necessary; improve their lot in life; and, finally, deny them their prior claim to the lands that the Mormons now occupied.[23] "It is our duty," Young had said, "to afford them every reasonable encouragement to acquire the habits of a peaceful, productive life, and in this the Lord will bless us and them."[24]

Young's claim of divine rights to the Indians' land was a concept the Indians could not accept, especially Walkara's Utes. The "Mormonees" were out and out intruders, and as such the Utes retaliated against the Mormons in the summer of 1853 with a continuing rash of depredations. Young's response was to implore his followers to practice restraint and to avoid hostilities wherever possible. His policy was difficult to enforce, however, and while Young preached a policy of defense and pacifism, his flock wanted to "kill every damn rascal."[25]

Young's relationship with Walkara had always been tenuous. In order to keep peace with the Utes, Young was forced to accede to Walkara's demands for gifts of various kinds. Although he wasn't forced to do so, Young fed and clothed the Indians. The funds to satisfy Walkara's demands as well as to fulfill Young's own desire to improve the Indians' welfare, properly should have come from Washington, Young believed, instead of from his own contingency funds.[26]

He had long complained bitterly to Washington that his annual salaries as both Superintendent of Indian Affairs and as governor were inadequate. The federal government, in addition, had put a clamp on his contingency account, an account that he wanted to use to help feed and clothe the Indians.[27] All along, Young undoubtedly had been waging a campaign to convince the Indians that it was the "Mericats" who were their enemies and those responsible for the poor quality of their lives, while it was he, Young, and the "Mormonees" who were their friends.

To make matters worse, Young was forced to perform humbling bureaucratic tasks—writing periodic status reports and submitting for approval vouchers for his meager expenditures. Meanwhile, the various territorial officers Washington sent to Utah immediately found themselves doing battle with the autocratic Young, and most refused to knuckle under to the Mormon oligarchy. Either they left Utah voluntarily or were sent back to Washington against their wishes. All these matters accounted for Young's feelings of bitterness toward the administration.[28]

Early in the summer of 1853, just before Walkara's war began, Captain John W. Gunnison and his surveying party began their trek westward in search of a transcontinental railroad route, knowing very little about the hostilities taking place between the Mormons and the Utes along the proposed expedition route.

Plans for a transcontinental railroad had been under continuous discussion in Congress. The lands between the Mississippi and the Pacific were largely unknown, uncharted. Transportation across the continent was extremely slow and inefficient, and mail service, at best, was irregular. The nation was experiencing growing pains, and a railroad to link the East and West was viewed as a vital step toward its growth.[29]

But first a survey would have to be conducted to find the best all-weather route. Jefferson Davis, Secretary of War under Franklin Pierce, had charge of the U.S. Army Corps of Engineers, and appointed Gunnison, a seasoned military surveyor, as the man for the job. In choosing Gunnison, Davis ignored the efforts of Senator Thomas Hart Benton to have his son-in-law, John Charles Fremont, already a national hero and an equally qualified military surveyor, appointed to head the expedition.[30,31]

While on a previous surveying mission in Utah, Gunnison first came up with the notion of a transcontinental railroad, and he had hoped to interest the government in the undertaking with Gunnison himself in command of the survey. His selection by Davis fulfilled a dream for this forty-one year old career officer. As Gunnison had described it, the idea of a railroad extending across the country "would be so wonderful in its result on trade and the destinies of the race that all other human efforts sink in insignificance before it."[32]

Gunnison's final expedition plan was drafted in May, 1853, and he set off immediately for the West. In his party were Creutzfeldt, the botanist; Kern, the artist and topographer; an astronomer; a surgeon and geologist; and approximately thirty mounted riflemen under the command of Captain R.M. Morris. The expedition's second in command was another military surveyor, Lieutenant Edward Griffin Beckwith.

The route of the survey was to follow the 38th and 39th parallels through the central West, on a direct line between St. Louis and San Francisco. It would provide the best and most efficient railroad passage between the Mississippi and the Pacific, and would pass through the Mormon settlements in Utah where Young and his flock were by now the largest group of people in the inter-mountain West.[33]

The idea of a railroad invading Young's private domain gave the prophet cause for concern, for it would speed the influx into the territory of non-friendly gentiles, the very ones from whom the Mormons had been running the previous few decades.

Gunnison was intelligent, ambitious and superbly qualified for his job. A West Pointer, he had graduated from the academy in 1837, at age twenty-five, second in a class of fifty.[34] He had developed his engineering and surveying skills in the southeast in the 1830s where he had participated in the Cherokee Indian removal to Oklahoma. He had helped survey the Michigan-Wisconsin boundaries in the 1840s. In 1849, he had surveyed the Great Salt Lake basin, and it was there that he first encountered the Latter-day Saints. He had lived among them, and his opinions of the sect were favorable.[35] These opinions were set forth in his book, *The Mormons In The Valley of the Great Salt Lake,* published in 1852.[36]

Gunnison had met Young during his previous Utah visit, and knowing something of the prophet's personality was shrewd enough to have written Young that he would be traversing Utah Territory and would be grateful for Young's cooperation and help.

Gunnison's journey through the central plains and across the Rockies was uneventful, but early in October, as the expedition reached Green River, Utah, a Ute Indian, Tewip Narrienta, who had just joined the expedition as a guide, suddenly left the Gunnison command, explaining that he was worried about the safety of his squaw and papoose. Narrienta had picked up the scent of trouble. The expedition was getting closer to Mormon settlements, and Lieutenant Beckwith perceived that this was the real cause of the Indian's concern. Narrienta had repeatedly warned Beckwith about the "Mormonees."[37]

Hostile flare-ups between the Mormons and the Utes were now occurring frequently, having increased during the time Gunnison had been working his way through Colorado and into

Utah. The most recent incident had occurred a week before the massacre. Gunnison had arrived at Manti, a Mormon settlement, where he was informed that the Utes had recently invaded the community, killing several of the residents, destroying their belongings and driving off the livestock.[38]

When the expedition reached Millard County, Utah,[39] Gunnison had stopped to visit with Bishop Call, an apostle of the church. Call informed Gunnison of the incident at Meadow Creek between the Pavants and the immigrants and the resultant death of Tonif, father of Moshoquop. Call had then gone on to explain that Moshoquop and a band of Pavant warriors had disappeared into the mountains, and he had warned Gunnison to be careful.[40]

Gunnison had taken Call's warning casually. During his previous visit to Utah, Gunnison had become friendly with both Kanosh and Moshoquop, and he had assured Call that no harm could come to him or to the men in the expedition. However, in his meeting with Call, Gunnison had assumed that Moshoquop knew that Gunnison was in the area. Moshoquop did not.[41]

The Gunnison expedition reached the Sevier River during the third week in October. One day, while encamped there, Gunnison took out his journal and, contemplating his accomplishments during the last several months, noted that "the great mountains have been passed...a great new road could [now] stretch across the continent." He was pleased with himself. It was his hope that upon reaching California, having successfully completed his mission, to resign his army commission and be appointed chief engineer for the railroad's construction.[42]

The Gunnison camp site was located at Pioneer Creek, along the Sevier River. As frequently happened on surveying missions, the expedition party split up, Gunnison, Creutzfeldt, Kern, Potter, Bellows and the three soldiers, Liptrott, Caulfield and Merteens, heading west along the Sevier, bound for Sevier Lake. In the meantime, Captain Morris, in charge of the riflemen, would take a small company of men to explore terrain in another direction. The rest of the expedition party would remain in camp at Pioneer Creek.[43]

Gunnison was never to complete the survey. In the early hours of October 26, 1853, an explosion of rifle fire had cut through the darkness along the Sevier. Gunnison and his seven companions were dead, their bodies stripped of their clothing and mutilated, survey notes scattered to the winds—victims not of the hostile Utes but of Young's favored tribe, the reputedly peaceful Pavants.

Moshoquop died at Deseret in 1893, forty years after the Gunnison massacre and within a few miles of where it happened. Only after his death was the Indians' version of the massacre told. It was related to Josiah F. Gibbs, editor of the *Millard County Blade*, by Mareer, an old Pavant Indian.

According to Mareer's account, the Indians had caught sight of the Gunnison party the day before the massacre, and from then on had carefully watched the party's movements while hiding in the willows along the banks of the Sevier. Throughout the night and into the early hours of October 26, the Gunnison group slept soundly, the Indians watching, waiting. Shortly before sunrise, William Potter, the guide, who was also the cook, lighted a fire. He placed an iron tripod and kettles over the fire, and was soon joined around the fire by Creutzfeldt and Kern.[44]

Presently, Gunnison arose and walked to the river to wash his hands and face. Then Moshoquop, suddenly emerging from his hiding place in the willows, signalled an order to the other Indians. A burst of rifle fire shattered the stillness of the fall morning. Kern, Creutzfeldt and Potter fell dead, fatally wounded by shots fired by Moshoquop, Mareer and the other Indians. At the sound of the gunfire, Gunnison ran back from the river bank. Unarmed, and quickly realizing that he couldn't stave off the Indians, he turned back in an effort to escape, and ran to the river in the midst of a flurry of arrows.[45]

The Indians ran after Gunnison, carefully searching the willows for their prey. It was not long until they came upon the captain's body, covered in blood, critically wounded by the arrows, but still alive. Seeing the Indians, Gunnison managed to raise himself to a sitting position, and extended his hands in an appeal to be spared. The Indians paused, as though they might actually spare Gunnison's life, when suddenly an Indian, Jimmy

Knights, known as a bad Indian, appeared in the willows. He stood over Gunnison for a moment, and then abruptly discharged his gun point blank at the captain. Gunnison sank back, dead.[46]

News of the Gunnison massacre gave rise to angry protests from newspapers throughout the country, demanding that the guilty parties immediately be brought to justice. The federal government, however, was slow to react, and it was not until the spring of 1854, nearly six months after Gunnison's death, that the administration took action. It ordered 300 soldiers and civilians, under the command of Colonel Edward Jenner Steptoe, to Utah to apprehend the murderers.[47] It was conceded that the perpetrators were the Pavant Indians, and that they had killed Gunnison and his men in reprisal for the death of Tonif at the hands of Abrams, the apostate Jew.

Steptoe's investigation met resistance at every turn, thwarted by Young, who insisted that the investigation be conducted through his Indian agency. In that way, Young would have final authority over the inquiry, one involving his favored tribe, the Pavants. Steptoe quickly saw that he would be operating without any real status. He was having the same kind of trouble with Young as the various federal officials in the territory had had. As always, Young had to be in full control.

The act of bringing Steptoe and his troops to Utah had so enraged Young and his followers that hostilities between the Mormons and Steptoe's soldiers was unavoidable. Steptoe's men didn't mask their contempt for the Mormons' polygamous ways, and the Mormons' allegiance to Young was so strong that their behavior was uncooperative and subversive. Complicating matters, Mormon women were strongly attracted to the soldiers, driving the Mormon elders frantic. Street violence, open clashes between the Mormons and the soldiers, happened frequently.[48]

Without Young's cooperation, Steptoe was forced to negotiate alone with Young's friend,

Kanosh, chief of the Pavants. Only after several months had passed was Steptoe finally able to apprehend eight "guilty" Indians. Of the eight that Kanosh turned over, only three were subsequently indicted by the territorial grand jury.[49]

The three indicted Indians were Ankle Joint, Sandy Hair and White Tree.[50] In Indian Mareer's version of the massacre, he had named several Indians as participants in the murders, including Moshoquop, Jimmy Knights and Mareer himself. There is no explanation of how Kanosh decided which eight Indians to turn over to Steptoe and why the participants named by Mareer did not include those Indians subsequently named in the indictment.[51]

The Indians were put on trial March 21, 1855 in Nephi City, Utah, in a crowded courtroom, before an all-Mormon jury. Presiding over the trial was Chief Territorial Justice John F. Kinney who, besides being the ranking jurist in Utah, also operated a boarding house which had come to be known as a favorite haunt for Steptoe's soldiers and their Mormon women friends.

Participating in the trial, in addition to Kinney, were Joseph Hollman, the prosecuting attorney, a hard-drinker who had a strong attraction to Indian women; Lieutenant Sylvester Mowrey, the assistant prosecuting attorney, a handsome, articulate and able young lawyer; Almon W. Babbitt, the defense attorney, a gifted orator, a "tool" of Young's but a man not fully trusted by the prophet.[52]

The defense built its case on the grounds that the Pavants, a sub-tribe of the Utes, were involved in Walkara's war against the Mormons, and thus against the United States. For that reason, the three accused Indians couldn't be tried as murderers since the Gunnison massacre was but another skirmish in the war.[53]

On the prosecution's side, two Mormons, John King and Daniel Thompson, had testified that they had helped bury the remains of the victims and had seen and talked with Ankle Joint and Sandy Hair, both of whom had freely admitted to participating in the murders.[54]

The most damaging testimony had come from an Indian woman named Midsummer who lived at the Pavant camp. On the night before the massacre, she told of a warrior entering the camp and telling of the arrival of a small band of "Mericats." Around noon of the day of the massacre, a Pavant war party, including the three accused, had returned to camp with plunder taken from the Gunnison party and had announced they had killed the "Mericats."[55]

After the evidence had been presented, Judge Kinney instructed the jury to return one of two possible verdicts, and no other: innocent, or guilty of murder in the first degree. No one doubted the outcome of the case since the testimony was so overwhelmingly against the accused. However, contrary to the judge's instructions and in opposition to the evidence, the all-Mormon jury returned a verdict of manslaughter.[56] The surprise verdict stunned the courtroom. Kinney was not bound to accept the verdict, but as he had later explained he knew immediately that the verdict was as good as he could possibly get from a Mormon jury. Kinney then sentenced the Indians to three years in the territorial prison at Salt Lake City, the maximum allowable sentence for manslaughter. Shorty after they were carted off to prison, the three Indians escaped. According to Young, the Indians were recaptured and served out their time, but only after his own intercession. He contended that the gentiles had made no effort to apprehend the Indians, better to build a case of complicity against the Mormons.[57]

The federal judge in Utah Territory who was most at odds with Young was Judge W.W. Drummond, a conscientious jurist with a weakness for women and cards, who presided over the federal district court at Fillmore. The Mormons war with Drummond began on the day of his arrival in Utah, and to this day the Mormon church is still at war with Drummond. When Drummond arrived in Utah, he was accompanied, according to foreign visitors, by "the lovely Ada, his concubine," and by his Negro servant, Cato.[58] To enter Young's puritanical stronghold in the company of a lady of doubtful virtue was cause enough to infuriate the prophet, but when Drummond openly defied the

Mormon-controlled court system in Utah, spurning Young's authority, the prophet's outrage reached fever pitch.[59] Young accused Drummond of having "transcended his authority" and of having "demeaned himself...like a dog or wolf, vicious and brutal, whining and snappish, vain as a peacock and ignorant as a jackass." Drummond, to Young, exemplified the "infernal, dirty, sneaking rotten-hearted politicians" Washington was sending to Utah, and Young vowed to get rid of "as many such white-livered, blackhearted, sycophantic demagogues as the administration shall send."[60]

It was during the November, 1855, term of Drummond's court in Fillmore that Levi Abrams was taken from Salt Lake City to Fillmore, the new territorial capital, to be tried for the "willful and unprovoked" murder of Tonif, the Pavant chieftain. In a replay of the Gunnison trial, Abrams, the Mormon Jew, was acquitted by an all-Mormon jury. The jury, Drummond had later written, was "true to the law of the Church and basely false to the law of the land..."[61]

Early in January, 1856, a few months after he was acquitted of Tonif's murder, Abrams was back in court again, this time as plaintiff in an assault case. The defendants were Judge W.W. Drummond himself, together with his black servant, Cato. According to one version of the story, an altercation had taken place between Abrams and the judge. It had occurred during a card game in which Drummond had lost money to Abrams. The two had quarreled, but Drummond had restrained himself. The next morning, however, Drummond had sent Cato to horsewhip the Jew. Abrams had sworn out a complaint, and both Drummond and his servant had been arrested and forced to appear in Drummond's own court before a judge whose jurisdiction Drummond had once denied.[62]

Relations between the Mormons and the federal troops had been severely strained before the Gunnison trial, but now, with the jury's verdict reached, relations were hopelessly ruptured. Steptoe, Kinney and other federal officials wrote bitter letters to their superiors in Washington. But it was Lieutenant Sylvester Mowrey, the assistant prosecuting attorney, whose protest made the strongest impact on the nation.[63] On March 29, 1855, Mowrey wrote a carefully worded letter to *The New York Times* and included an account of the trial. There was no official transcript of the trial. The only record was the one Mowrey himself had kept.

In his letter to the newspaper, Mowrey accused Young of manipulating the jury and using the influence of Young's office to obstruct justice. Outraged, Mowrey called the trial "a wanton insult to the friends of the lamented dead," and called for doing away with Utah Territory and dividing it between Nebraska, New Mexico and California. Nearly two months after it was sent, Mowrey's letter appeared on the front page of *The New York Times* under the headline: "Trial of the Indian Murderers of Captain Gunnison. Verdict of Manslaughter Only. Mormon Interference With The Cause of Justice. Infamous Dictation of Brigham Young."[64]

It is worth noting that Mowrey at the time was having an affair with Young's daughter-in-law,[65] and it is reasonable to assume that the prophet was aware of the liaison and that the affair had been an issue between Mowrey and Young prior to the trial.

Young's reputation had become seriously tarnished. His squabbles with the administration regarding his autonomy in Utah had tested Washington's patience. The outbreak of violence between his followers and the federal troops had further sullied his image. And now with accusations of a rigged jury in the Gunnison trial, Young fell into national disfavor.

Adding to the prophet's woes, rumors were now circulating that the Mormons, beyond rigging the jury, were actually in league with the Indians in perpetrating the massacre, or else, with faces painted to look like Indians, had actually killed Gunnison and his companions themselves. The rumors intensified with the news that the convicted Indians had somehow managed to escape from the territorial prison. Whatever Young's role had been in the murders, the belief was widely held that Young was deeply implicated in a plot to defy the authority of the federal government, or even something worse.

In the meantime, Judge Drummond, outraged by the juridiction of Mormon-controlled judges and by his own humiliation in the Abrams assault case, resigned his appointment. In his letter of resignation, which was published in *The New York Times* April 14, 1857, he charged that Captain Gunnison's murder had been committed under the direction of the Mormons. The news thundered across the nation for it had reinforced the rumors that had been bruited about since the trial ended.

Drummond's charges eventually reached Gunnison's widow who wrote Drummond for a further explanation of his charges. In her letter, she said that she had the impression all along that "the Mormons were the directors of my husband's murder," notwithstanding the fact that she had a letter of condolence from Brigham Young.[66] Drummond responded two weeks later. In his letter to Mrs. Gunnison, which also was printed in *The New York Times*, Drummond claimed that proof of Mormon guilt was made plain to him in Abrams's trial for Tonif's murder, and that it had confirmed what was already evident to him in the Gunnison trial—that the massacre was "a deeply and maturely laid plan" by the Mormons to murder all the men on the Gunnison expedition and to blame the Indians. Drummond further claimed that, according to the evidence, certain Mormons had actually fired most of the fatal shots. He went on to accuse, by name, nine Mormons who had assisted the Indians in the massacre.[67]

One of them was Levi Abrams.[68]

In answer to the charges, Young began compiling evidence to deny Mormon involvement. He deposed jurors, various officials, and spectators at the trial, offering along with twenty pages of sworn statements his own opinions about the trial. In a sixty-six page document, which he sent to Jefferson Davis,[69] he gave a complete history of the trial along with his version of the massacre and the events leading up to it. He concluded that since the murder of Gunnison and his men took place at the time of Walkara's war, the Indians couldn't be convicted of first degree murder, this in support of the claim of defense attorney, Almon Babbitt. He pointed out that if a gentile jury had tried the Indians, the trial would have been grossly unfair, owing to the gentiles' anti-Mormon bias. He conceded that the jury had not complied with Judge Kinney's instructions, but questioned why the judge had accepted the jury's verdict as final.[70]

In January of 1855, Colonel Steptoe was appointed by Franklin Pierce to succeed Young as governor. Pierce had sufficient cause for replacing Young, over and above the Gunnison matter. The practice of polygamy was repugnant to the people of the United States, and Young, as high priest of the custom, couldn't be permitted to occupy his post without it seeming to be an endorsement of the practice by the administration. In addition, Young, on numerous occasions, had taunted the federal government from the pulpit by preaching that only the Almighty could remove him as governor; that any replacement for him would be lynched; and that he would declare war against the United States if it attempted to replace him. The administration couldn't let Young's swaggering go unchallenged.[71]

Steptoe, after receiving Pierce's appointment as governor, concluded that as a non-Mormon governor of a territory heavily populated with Mormons he would be saddled with insurmountable problems, especially with Young around as the real power. Steptoe reasoned that only a Mormon could govern Utah Territory, regretfully declined the commission, and left the territory in 1855, never to return. Young had prevailed—but only temporarily.[72]

President James Buchanan, a Democrat, had succeeded Franklin Pierce in the 1856 election. A national issue in the campaign was Utah Territory—specifically, the rebellion of Brigham Young and the Mormons against the United States as well as the practice of polygamy, an institution which most of the country found reprehensible. Buchanan had taken a strong stand on both issues, vowing to put an end to the Mormons' plural marriages and to their insurgent conduct.

Buchanan, realizing that the Mormons would not accept a new governor without force, ordered General William S. Harney to invade the territory with 2,500 troops in order to ensure the installation of his new gubernatorial appointee, Alfred Cumming of Georgia.[73] Buchanan, however, had failed to notify Young that he was being replaced, and Young immediately suspected that the Utah invasion was based upon religious bias and was but another attempt to drive the Mormons away from their homes as had happened so many times in the past.[74]

In August, 1857, Young issued his "Citizens of Utah" proclamation, essentially declaring war against the United States. He declared martial law in the territory, and stood ready to repel the invasion. He mustered the Mormon Minute Men, his elite guard, to harass the oncoming troops, and ordered the Nauvoo Legion, the Mormon army, to face the federal troops head on. A day after the invasion, Young had said:

> What are they angry at me for? Because I reprove men for their iniquity, and because I have such influence here—the very thing they are all after...There is no influence, truth or righteousness in the world, only what flows from God our Father in the heavens...
>
> What is the news circulating throughout the United States? That Captain Gunnison was killed by Brigham Young...That Brigham Young has killed all the men who have died between the Missouri river and California...Such reports are in the bellows, and editors and publishers are blowing them out...[75]

Young's words, mocking as they were, proved prophetic. In what was one of the most tragic episodes in Mormon history, 150 California-bound immigrants, men, women and children, gentiles all, travelling through southern Utah by wagon-train, were slaughtered in cold blood by the Mormons in what has come to be known as the Mountain Meadows massacre. In the Mormon version of the story, the Indians, convinced that the "Mericats" were after them, attacked the wagon train on their own volition. The Mormons, living in the immediate area, had seen the

Indians attacking the "Mericats" and mistakenly concluded that their sect was in league with the Indians in the slaughter, as they had been in other past conflicts with the "Mericats."[76]

But in another version, it was the Mormon settlers who had instigated the attack, the Indians in the area blindly supporting the "Mormonees" in the murders.[77]

Mrs. Ann Eliza Young, the prophet's nineteenth wife, in commenting on the Mountain Meadows massacre, excoriated her husband: "As far as I'm concerned," she wrote, "I believe all the murders lie at his door...his hands are red with innocent blood, his garments dyed with it, and no atonement can ever wipe out the damning spots."[78]

A Methodist minister, in a lecture delivered in 1876 from his pulpit in Salt Lake City, condemned Young for using the Indians as his scapegoats. "Lo! the poor Indians!" he said. "If they were guilty of a hundreth part of the crimes which Brigham attributes to them, they would be worse fiends than the most rabid Indian hater ever estimated them to be."

Young had long manipulated the Indians. He depicted the "Mormonees" as the good-guys, the "Mericats" as the bad-guys. He tried to convince the Indians that the federal troops, having now invaded Utah, were the enemy, and warned the Indians to side with the Mormons. Chief Walkara, understanding well the conflict between Young and the administration, began playing the same game as the prophet, manipulating Young by threatening to join in with the federal troops, now under the command of General Albert Sidney Johnston.

There is considerable basis for speculating that Young, in the Gunnison massacre, may have convinced the Pavants that the Gunnison expedition was a threat to their tribe, and that their safety and welfare could best be realized with Gunnison out of the way.

That's how things were in Utah Territory in the turbulent 1850s.

Months had passed before Alfred Cumming was finally accepted as governor. Eventually Young capitulated, relinquishing his post as governor and as Superintendent of Indian Affairs in return for a peaceful withdrawal in 1858 of the federal troops.

The identity of the real perpetrators of the Gunnison massacre, whether Indians, Mormons, or both, would forever remain a mystery.

After Gunnison's death, Lieutenant Edward Griffin Beckwith went on to complete the survey for the railroad, and Gunnison's dream of a "great new road...across the continent" was realized in 1869 with the completion of the Union Pacific.

Almon W. Babbitt, the defense attorney, having quarreled with Young after the trial, started off across the plains in 1855, but was murdered by the Indians. "He lived a fool and died a fool," Young had said. "He undertook to quarrel with me and was soon after killed by the Indians."[80]

Joseph Hollman, the prosecuting attorney whose weakness was Indian women, picked up a venereal infection from a squaw on the day after the verdict was handed down. After being treated in Salt Lake City, he left Utah Territory forever.[81]

Chief Territorial Justice John F. Kinney, who registered a strong protest to the administration over Young's interference with the Gunnison jury, eventually compromised with the Mormons, better to ensure his future in Utah.[82]

Lieutenant Sylvester Mowrey, the assistant prosecuting attorney, settled in Arizona, and ran the prosperous Mowrey silver mines, later becoming a member of the U.S. Boundary Commission.[83]

Judge W.W. Drummond took up residence in Chicago in 1857, shortly after resigning his post in Utah; and Levi Abrams, the Jew who became a Mormon and triggered Utah's most explosive decade, was last heard from in 1874, operating a saloon on Temple Square in Salt Lake City.[84,85]

Brigham Young, the prophet, died in 1877. Long before that he had sent a lock of Captain Gunnison's hair to the soldier's widow in Bethlehem, Pennsylvania.[86]

Chapter 5

SAMUEL AND JOSEPH

Late in 1866,[1] a young man on horseback rode into the Creek nation in what is now the eastern half of Oklahoma. His only possessions of value were a pouch of gold coins, stuffed into his saddlebag, his white horse, and an official looking envelope on which he was staking his future in America. It contained a license, issued by Carl Shurz, Secretary of the Interior, permitting him to trade with the Indians. In return, he had posted a $10,000 bond with the government, pledging he would deal honestly and squarely with the various tribes residing in Indian Territory,[2] a pledge he would never violate.

The Civil War had recently ended. The railroads, which would bring booming commercial activity and a swarm of white settlers to the area, would come years later. But for now, the land was barren and unsettled, populated by only a handful of non-Indians. The rider, who had journeyed from St. Louis, was a twenty-six year old Jew, one of the first of his faith to come to Oklahoma.[3] His name was Joseph Sondheimer, and he was destined to become a successful wholesaler of hides and furs and one of Muskogee, Oklahoma's leading citizens. Sondheimer operated his hide business without stop until his death in 1913 when it was taken over by his two sons, Samuel and Alexander. When the business was finally dissolved in 1942, it had been in operation for seventy-six years, and was one of the oldest continuously operated businesses in Oklahoma.[4]

The Sondheimer family left Muskogee long ago but their imprint on the community still remains. A stained glass window with Sondheimer's name and date of death (July 10, 1913) inlaid in the glass, graces Beth Ahaba Congregation at 7th and Boston street.[5] The old Sondheimer hide house still stands at 2nd and Fondulac Street alongside the tracks of the "Katy," the old Missouri, Kansas and Texas Railroad.[6] A plaque in the foyer of the YMCA at Sixth and Court honors Alexander Sondheimer and his wife; for they left a large part of their estate to the YMCA and YWCA.[7] In the archives of the First National Bank of Muskogee is a dusty photograph of the Bank's board of directors, circa 1925, in which Sam Sondheimer with slicked back hair and high collar stares glumly at the camera.[8]

The land into which Joseph Sondheimer rode in 1866 was set aside exclusively for the Indians of the southeast. Congress, in 1830, under Andrew Jackson's administration, enacted the "Indian Removal Bill," calling for the Five Civilized Tribes—the Creeks, Choctaws, Cherokees, Chickasaws and Seminoles—to be transplanted from their prosperous farmlands in the gulf states to a gigantic tract of land west of the Mississippi, or to what is now the state of Oklahoma.

Jackson had been elected president on the strength of his promise to drive the Indians out of their lands in Mississippi, Georgia, Alabama, Florida and the Carolinas. In this way, more lands could be provided for the increasing number of white settlements springing up along the eastern seaboard. Under terms of the treaty with the government, the Indians exchanged their rich farms and orchards, acre for acre, for new lands in the West, taking their black slaves with them. Their journey to the West, the infamous "Trail of Tears," as it came to be known, was long and fraught with misery. Many of their number died during the ordeal. But the Five Tribes, once settled, gradually began rebuilding their lives in a strange and barren land, building new homes, carefully cultivating the soil.

The land in the West was given to the Five Tribes in perpetual ownership, a land, Andrew Jackson had promised, that "should be theirs so long as the grass grew and the rivers flowed."[9] Conditions, in addition, were set down by the government to give the tribes the right to their own systems of government as well as nominal authority over non-Indians. Whites were permitted on Indian lands for trapping and trading, as Sondheimer was. The land was known officially as Indian Territory, and special non-Indian citizens were required to heed the laws of the various tribes. However, ultimate authority over the Indians was granted to the U.S. Indian superintendents and agents, and hence the true power rested in the hands of the government. A predictable outcome of this double bind was that the Indians had no real or just means of protecting themselves against non-Indians. It was an untenable position because they had no redress against either civil or criminal transgressions by the white man.

The Civil War in 1861 didn't do well by the Five Tribes. The homes they had built more than thirty years before were burned. Their fields were stripped bare and laid waste. Now impoverished, they were dealt still another blow. They had tried to take a neutral stand in the war even though they were southerners and slave-holders. But the pressures to remain neutral were too strong. Some of the Indians eventually succumbed to the entreaties of the half-breeds among them as well as to those of the whites residing in Arkansas—all anti-abolitionists. Most of the Choctaws and Chickasaws joined up with the Confederacy, while many but not all of the Seminoles, Cherokees and Creeks sided with the Union. As punishment for the defection of some, all five tribes at the end of the war were forced to enter into a treaty with the government calling for the surrender to the government of the western half of their domain in return for payment of fifteen to thirty cents an acre. The land ceded to the government became the Oklahoma Territory, and was used for the settlement of other tribes, both friendly and hostile. The unruly Cheyenne, Arapaho, Apache, Comanche, Wichita and

Kiowa were assigned reservations here, and the blood of both whites and Indians was spilled as the government attempted to effect the new land allocation. Other more friendly tribes were also assigned reservations in Oklahoma Territory, among them the Ponca, Pawnee, Osage, Kickapoo and Potawatomi.

Separating Oklahoma Territory from Indian Territory was a strip of unassigned land, setting apart the Five Tribes, now consolidated into the eastern area, from the numerous tribes on reservations in the western area. The strip of land, to be known as Oklahoma Land, would, twenty-three years later, be opened helter-skelter to white settlers in a wild and lawless scramble for land. It would gain notoriety as the sensational "Run" of 1889.

The Five Tribes, now dividing up the eastern half of Oklahoma, began to resume their normal lives, putting the war behind them. The war had taken an especially heavy toll on the Creeks who had lost large herds of cattle, but resolutely they set about re-building, even improving, their herds. Doggedly, they began re-cultivating their farmlands, and within a few years were producing an abundant supply of corn, wheat, oats, rice and potatoes. Orchards of apples, peaches and plums now surrounded their rebuilt farmhouses, and experiments in growing cotton and tobacco met with some measure of success among these talented agriculturists.

Each tribe was allotted its own land within Indian Territory. The Creek nation, where Sondheimer settled, was located in the east central section, between the Cherokees to the north and the Choctaws to the south. The present locations of Tulsa, Muskogee and Okmulgee were included in the domain of the Creek nation.

Even though Congress enacted laws to protect the Five Tribes' lands against the intrusion of white settlers, the whites, in defiance of the law, began to intrude nonetheless. The only laws on the books were those enacted and enforced by the Indians. No Federal laws existed for the regulation of the lives of the whites.[10] As a result, Indian Territory became a haven for outlaws and misfits.

In 1869, the Creeks would elect as their principal chief, Samuel Checote, a man who was committed to preserving the racial integrity of the Indian and to preventing the further intrusion of unauthorized whites into Indian lands. He was a man in striking contrast to Sondheimer—tall, well-educated, a soft-spoken Confederate army hero, all of the things Sondheimer was not. The lives of the two men intersected only briefly through an exchange of correspondence, but beyond that their paths did not cross. They were a generation apart in age and a world apart in culture and attitude, one a Jew, the other a full-blood Creek. But despite these highly-visible differences, they shared some deeper characteristics: both men had great physical and moral courage; and both were immigrants, transplanted to an alien and desolate land—Sondheimer from his home in Bavaria, Checote from the rich orchards and magnolia-shaded streams of the peaceful Chattahoochee valley in Alabama. If things had been otherwise, the two men might have been friends. But, sadly, they were destined to be in conflict with each other. It had to be so. No other two men symbolized so clearly the conflicting attitudes and objectives of Indian and white man in the late nineteenth century as did these outstanding men—Sondheimer, the quintessential white man, pushing for statehood, for greater western expansion, and for a better life in the West—and Checote, the quintessential Indian, deploring all the things Sondheimer believed in, hating the dreaded Iron Horse, futilely trying to protect the rights of his people from the rapid incursion of the white settler.

Sondheimer, like most early settlers in the West, was a practical-minded man. His sole mission was survival, to seek out economic opportunities wherever he could find them. His motives were not unusual for an immigrant in a new land, for no such opportunities were open to him in the old country. But now, in the developing West, he was confronted at almost every turn by potentially lucrative trading opportunities. All that any man needed, especially one as single-minded as Sondheimer, was a bit of working capital, the ability to spot a commercial opportunity when it appeared, and an enormous amount of physical courage. On all three counts, he was amply prepared when he first rode into the Creek nation.

Joseph Sondheimer was born in Valkerschleir, Bavaria, in 1840. When he arrived in America as a boy of twelve in 1852, he moved in with a family named Rayner in Baltimore, old friends of the Sondheimers from Germany. His early life on the eastern seaboard is not well documented; however, it is known that he eventually left Baltimore and took up residence briefly in Columbus, Pennsylvania, before eventually moving west to St. Louis before the outbreak of the Civil War.[11]

During the war, Sondheimer travelled as a peddler around Memphis and Cairo, selling various types of merchandise to Union soldiers, and presumably engaging in a variety of other commercial ventures at the same time, either alone or with partners. His home was St. Louis for about twelve years, from before the Civil War until 1872. During this time he married, joined the United Hebrew Temple, and fathered five children, only two of whom survived, his sons Samuel and Alexander.

While residing in St. Louis, Sondheimer was away from home frequently, making numerous forays into Indian Territory on his white horse, buying for cash hides and furs from the Indians and shipping them back to eastern markets. There is some evidence to suggest that prior to his official move to Indian Territory in 1872, he had already become successful enough to build depots to warehouse the produce he had obtained from the various tribes. The depots were situated along the military trail that led from Fort Scott, Kansas, to Jefferson, Texas.[12] His goods were eventually routed east by steamboat from the U.S. Army post at Fort Gibson via the Arkansas River.[13]

In 1870, work had begun on the Missouri, Kansas and Texas Railroad, and by the following year tracks had been laid from St. Louis, across the Arkansas River, into the northeast corner of the present Oklahoma. The "Katy," which was to be constructed along a south-southeast course through Oklahoma and into Texas would cross an established overland freighters' route at Fort Davis, I.T. The town was so named because it was just a short distance from the Confederate army fort of the same name which had been destroyed during the Civil War.[14]

Sondheimer and other merchants were making plans to erect stores to capitalize on the coming of the railroad to Fort Davis. It was expected that the point where the railroad crossed the overland freighters' route would become an important terminus where freight from the railroad would be exchanged to teamsters' outfits. Sondheimer, quick to act on opportunities, immediately petitioned the Commissioner of Indian Affairs for a permit to bring his family into Indian Territory and to reside in Fort Davis. His business interests in the southwest had developed to a point where it was no longer feasible to reside in St. Louis.[15]

The grade at Fort Davis, as it turned out, was too steep to construct a railroad station, so the "Katy" relocated the station at the top of the grade, somewhat farther away. The new location would be named "Muscogee," a name applied synonymously to the people of the Creek nation. This was the year 1872, the year Muskogee was founded[16] and the year Joseph Sondheimer, his wife and their two children, boarded the stage in Rolla, Missouri, bound for Fort Smith, Fort Gibson and a little settlement of tents and shacks called Muskogee.[17]

In addition to his hide and fur trading, Sondheimer took a job as commercial solicitor for the "Katy" while it was still under construction. He would ride through Texas on his white horse, heralding the news of the coming of the railroad and urging settlers to be ready with their freight shipments when the railroad eventually arrived. He had done his job well because thousands of tons of freight were awaiting shipment on the return run when the "Katy" finally arrived in Texas.[18]

Sondheimer, in the meantime, was doing well as a fur trader. Even before his permanent move to Muskogee, he had become a familiar figure, riding his white horse through Indian country. He would carry in his saddlebags thousands of dollars in gold coins which he paid to the Indians on the spot for various types of animal pelts—bear, deer, beaver, otter, wolf, coon, fox and possum.[19] His territory extended from Fort Sill on the west to Fayetteville, Arkansas, on the east, from Kansas to the north and

Texas to the south. Most of his trading, however, was in the Creek, Cherokee and Chickasaw nations, with an occasional trip to the reservations of the peaceful Osage, Fox, Sac and Shawnee tribes where he regularly secured large quantities of buffalo robes.[20]

In spite of the rampant lawlessness on the plains, Sondheimer never carried a weapon in his travels, and, despite an occasional encounter with an unfriendly Indian, was never robbed and never harmed. During his life in the West, he always had the respect of the Indian, and was, in fact, welcomed cordially by all the full-bloods wherever he went in the territory.[21]

Once the "Katy" reached Muskogee, Sondheimer's hide and fur business quickly began to prosper. Shipments to St. Louis, where Sondheimer's furs were processed, could be made faster and at less cost than by steamboat. Furthermore, transportation from St. Louis to eastern markets was becoming more efficient, but, more significant, the U.S. population was increasing at a healthy rate and, along with it, the need by consumers for more fur and leather goods.

By the early 1880s, the hides and furs Sondheimer was buying from the Indians had found an international market, and were being exported to central Europe.[22] An early pictorial record shows Sondheimer in 1883, accompanied by his twelve-year old son, Samuel, preparing a shipment in Muskogee of 10,000 pounds of deerskins, earmarked for one Sigmund Frank of Leipzig, Germany.[23]

As his business prospered, so did Sondheimer's standing in the commercial and social life of Muskogee. His hide exporting activities were given full praise in the Muskogee newspaper.

> Friday last, Mr. Joseph Sondheimer, of this city, shipped direct to Hamburg, Germany, via, New York and Liverpool, 1,680 deer skins, equal to 6,000-pounds. This is the first shipment Mr. Sondheimer has made this season. It will be followed by others later on. These 1,680 deer skins were all purchased by Mr. Sondheimer from Territory points, and were a fine and valuable assortment. Mr. Sondheimer is the great hide and fur man of the southwest and as he exports

his furs direct to the consumer he gets the best price and is enabled in consequence to pay the best price to the trappers, hunters and others who have fur to sell.[24]

In a follow-up story, the newspaper reported that Sondheimer "handled four-fifths of all Indian Territory hides and furs."[25]

In interviews with early settlers, conducted by the late Grant Foreman, the Oklahoma historian, the Sondheimer name turns up frequently with respect to various hide and fur transactions with local merchants, indicating that Sondheimer had various secondary sources of supply. One Albert Berry, an early settler, born in 1871, recalls working for the firm of Blackstone and Hays in Illinois Station, I.T. in 1888. The firm was in the mercantile business, and bought furs and hides direct from the Indians. Berry once bought ten otter and four beaver hides from an Indian named Sam Jumper. He paid Jumper five dollars for each hide, and then re-sold them for ten dollars each to young Sam Sondheimer who was buying hides for his father.[26]

An early settler named A. J. Kennedy, who had been in the mercantile business at the town of Sandy in the Chickasaw nation, recalls that he had sold only some of his merchandise to the Indians for cash, but had sold most in exchange for hides and furs. Kennedy eventually converted the hides and furs back to cash by selling them to "a Mr. Haas" (Julius Haas), a brother-in-law of Joseph Sondheimer. Haas was a trader in the small town of Atoka, I.T., in the Chickasaw nation.[27]

It is interesting to note that Sondheimer used his own hides and furs for barter. One Mary Francis Wood related to Foreman that while living in Muskogee she knew of two Chinese in the town who made dishes and vases from clay and traded them to Sondheimer for hides and furs.[28]

In his quest for hides, Sondheimer, in another instance, offered three dollars each for the two best beef hides brought to the International Fair held in Muskogee in 1880. And at yet another time, Sondheimer, during the big winter freeze of 1890,[29] bought for their hides all of the frozen cattle between Muskogee and Okmulgee, paying the Indians $1 for each of the dead animals.[30]

Julius Haas had married the sister of Sondheimer's wife, and it is to be presumed that the primitive life in Indian Territory was made more bearable for both women by their being near to each other. The records reveal nothing, but at some point Sondheimer's marriage was dissolved, his wife apparently returning to live in St. Louis.[31]

By now, Sondheimer's business had grown to a point where the establishment of another hide house became necessary. The year it was established isn't known; however, it was located in the town of Wagoner, in the Creek nation, a short distance north of Muskogee. As late as 1907, the year in which Oklahoma became a state, the townspeople of Wagoner had had their fill of it and petitioned the City Council to have the hide house shut down:

> To the Hon. Mayor and
> City Council of City of Wagoner
>
> Gentlemen:
>
> We the undersigned residents and taxpayers of city of
> Wagoner respectfully state that the Sondheimer hide house
> situated on the South side of West Cherokee Street in said
> city of Wagoner, is kept in such shape and condition and
> emits such an offensive odor as to make life miserable to us
> and we pray our honorable body to declare said house and
> business a nuisance and have the same removed and we will
> ever pray.[32]

Sondheimer's commercial success had gained his family social acceptance in Muskogee as evidenced by the following item in the town's newspaper in 1892:

> Today is Sammie Sondheimer's twenty-first birthday and he
> received a valuable present from his father and brother
> while celebrating the event quietly and properly in the
> circle of a few of his nearest friends. Sam is a good catch
> and probably it is not necessary for the Phoenix to remind
> the young ladies of Muskogee that this is leap year.[33]

Sondheimer was one of the founders of Beth Ahaba Congregation, but was not especially active in Jewish affairs in Muskogee. Neither were his children. In 1885, his oldest son, Alexander, married Eudora Cobb who was part Cherokee and one of the founding members of the Muskogee Embroidery Club.[34] In 1923, Alexander and his wife were killed in an auto accident in Nice, France, while on a pleasure trip. In his will, he left $150,000 each to the Muskogee YMCA and YWCA. He also left $50,000 each to the Boy Scouts, United Charities, the Presbyterian Church and Beth Ahaba.[35]

Before Sondheimer arrived in Indian Territory, Samuel Checote was already a leader and guiding force among the Creeks and a man of strong influence in the inner councils of the other civilized tribes. This quiet and statesmanlike man was passionately consumed by his love of God and by his desire to preach the gospel of Methodism to his people. As an ordained elder of the Methodist church, his religious beliefs played a strong part not only in the way he conducted his own life but in the way he presided over the Creek nation during his 12 years as principal chief.

Checote's entire life was rooted in Methodism. His parents had come under the influence of the white missionaries while they still lived in the south, and enrolled their son in a Methodist boarding school near Fort Mitchell, Alabama, in the fall of 1828.[36] Shortly after their arrival in the West in 1830, they sent young Samuel to Asbury School near the Oklahoma town now known as Eufala. It too was a Methodist boarding school, named in honor of the first Methodist bishop in America.[37]

Checote, who was born in 1819 in Chattahoochie valley, Alabama, was a boy of thirteen when he arrived in Indian Lands. The Checote family, like many Creeks, were well-off and comparatively well-educated, living as aristocrats in the south, on prosperous farms, in comfortable houses, all of their needs attended to by their black slaves. It can be assumed that the presence of Methodism in the West, which was then promulgated by Uncle John Harrell, a pioneer of Methodism in Indian Territory, was a familiar link with the past for young Checote, the only such connection he could make between his new home in the West and his old home in Alabama. It was little wonder that religious life took on such importance to the young Indian.

In 1852, when Sondheimer arrived in America as a boy of twelve, Samuel Checote, then thirty-three, had joined the Indian Mission Conference of the Methodist Episcopal Church, South, and was appointed to preach among his people at Little River, I.T.[38] In 1854 he was ordained deacon and appointed to the Methodist North Fork circuit; and five years later, in 1859, he was elected and ordained an elder, continuing as a circuit-riding preacher until the Civil War erupted in 1861.[39]

Checote, while preaching the gospel, was even then deeply involved in the affairs of the Creek nation, and most especially in guarding the racial integrity of his people against white immigration. His counsel was sought out frequently by both the Indians and the government, and despite his prominence as a political figure he never compromised his religious principles. His religious convictions were so strong, in fact, that once, during his tenure as principal chief, he was asked by a government agent to meet the agent at Tallequah, I.T., the capitol of the Cherokee nation, on an important Indian matter. Checote, however, failed to arrive on the appointed day, a Monday. He arrived instead on Tuesday, one day late. The angry Indian agent demanded an explanation. Checote apologized and said: "Had I arrived here on Monday, it would have been necessary for me to have travelled all day Sunday. This I could not do because I believe it wrong to use the day that way."[40]

Checote enlisted in the Confederate army in August, 1861, entering as a captain of company B, First Regiment, Creek Mounted Volunteers, and within the year had been elevated to the rank of Lt. Colonel.[41] There was no question as to where Checote's allegiances lay. He was a southerner, first and always, and the customs and traditions of the south were an integral part of his makeup. He was, moreover, a preacher in the southern branch of the Methodist church which was partial to the cause of the Confederacy; and, finally, because the Indian affairs of the government were under the supervision of southerners, it only made good sense for one as astute politically as Checote to side with the forces that could do the most for the Indians.[42]

Checote had distinguished himself as a soldier. His Creek regiment, while a part of the First Indian Cavalry Brigade of the Confederate army, attacked a federal supply train between Fort Scott, Kansas, a Union supply depot, and Fort Gibson. The train was made up of 300 wagons, carrying military supplies as well as supplies for settlers and traders. Goods and military equipment were valued at $1.5 million. Checote's capture of the supply train was a tremendous boost to the Confederate cause.[43]

When the war ended, Checote picked up where he left off, serving once again as a circuit rider and presiding elder in the Indian Mission. However, his influence among his people had grown. The Creek nation was divided during the Civil War, some Indians siding with the North, others with the South. With the war over, Checote took steps to bind up the old wounds. "The Muskogee people," he said, "should unite and live as one Nation, and those who were North during the late war were not to be called Northern people and those who were South were not to be Southern people; in short, there was to be no North and no South among the Muskogee people but peace and friendship."[44]

In 1869, Checote was elected principal chief, serving three consecutive four-year terms in the post. The Creeks had three departments of government under their constitution: the executive, headed by the principal chief whose duties were similar to those of the governor of an American state; the legislative, comprised of the House of Kings (their version of the Senate) and the House of Warriors (House of Representatives); and, finally, the judicial, consisting of a Supreme Court and district courts.

The coming of the railroad into Indian Territory had brought with it various white man interests seeking a break-down of the Indian governments. The white man was pounding at the Indian's door with ever-increasing force, and with each session of Congress came the possibility that new laws would be enacted that would hasten the opening of the gates to Indian Territory.[45]

Checote, in one of his first official acts as chief, called a council of all the civilized tribes to meet at Okmulgee, the capitol of the Creek nation, to try to curb "the adventurous spirit of the white man."[46] Checote understood fully the white man's culture and knew how to thwart his schemes. On the other hand, the white man found it difficult to understand Checote. As a full-blood, his manner was stoical, and his threshold of tolerance so high as to totally befuddle the white man. Nevertheless, his passion for protecting Indian Lands against the influx of whites consumed him nearly as much as his religion. Until his death he fought hard to maintain the rights of his people, ruling as chief with a firm and patient hand.

The Indian Journal, a newspaper distributed throughout Indian Territory, had this to say about Checote in its issue of June 15, 1876:

> Col. Sam Checote..is a good farmer, plants early and boasts none about his crops..40 acres standing corn, large and well-tilled vegetable garden. Full-blood Muscogee, tall well-built manly looking, a warrior in form but with an eye looking peace and good will to all. Few his equal as man and Christian. Good orator and preacher. Speaks English very well. Giving his children best education Nation offers.[47]

Captain F. B. Severs, a white man who lived among the Creeks and served for a time as Checote's secretary, said of the Chief: "I have lived a long time and met many men, but I have found no greater mind than his."[48] To General U.S. Grant, a wartime foe, Checote was "the greatest Indian I have ever met."[49]

Joseph Sondheimer and Samuel Checote might have lived out their lives without ever crossing each other's path. They might have but for one particular circumstance that brought them together. Non-citizens of Indian Territory who were engaged in business were required to pay a trading tax to the various tribes. Each tribe had its own tax schedule, and presumably the tax rates changed with some frequency. With the Creeks, dealers in patent medicines, lumber, dry goods, provisions and hardware, whose costs were known and shown on invoices, were taxed at a fixed rate on the first cost of goods brought into the nation for trade. The rate was roughly one percent, although rate changes varied with the chief serving at the time. [50]

Service businesses or other retail establishments, where costs couldn't be determined accurately, were taxed a fixed annual dollar amount. In 1900, for example, a barber shop with one chair paid $5 per year; with two chairs, $7.50. A dentist having a diploma paid $25; a restaurant, $10; a gunsmith, $6; a shooting gallery, $12; an ice cream or lemonade stand, $6. The highest annual dollar tax rates were levied against three classes of business: hotels, insurance agents, and "on each dealer in hides, peltry, furs, wool, pecans and other country produce."[51] In each of these cases, the tax was $50 per year. High as this tax may have been for hide dealers, Checote's successors were far more generous than Checote himself. Twenty years earlier, Checote extracted a tax of $100 from Sondheimer. It was this tax bill, both in amount and conception, that brought about a confrontation between Checote and Sondheimer.

It should be noted that early in 1884, shortly after Checote's death, the population of all of Indian Territory was 90,000, the Five Tribes in their entirety accounting for only 65,000 in a land set aside exclusively for them. In addition to the Indians, there were 12,000 whites with permits as tenants and farm laborers; 2,000 licensed traders, railroad employees and government employees and "several thousand sojourners, transients and intruders."[52] Essentially, then, 25,000, or nearly thirty percent, of the residents of Indian Territory were non-citizens, and the Indians stood by amazed and helpless as white interlopers staked out their land claims on Indian soil. If Checote's tax schedule was exhorbitant and established as a means of retarding commercial progress and thus the influx of more whites, then it was understandable. From Sondheimer's standpoint, however, the tax was grossly unfair, and as a result he became an outspoken critic of Indian-actuated taxation until the time Oklahoma achieved statehood.

On June 28, 1880, in a long, carefully worded letter to Checote, Sondheimer eloquently pleaded his case:

Honorable Samuel Chicote [sic]
Principle [sic] Chief, Muskogee Nation,
Okmulgee, Indian Territory

Dear Sir!

I hereby respectfully inform you, that a Tax Collector, so-called Lighthorse Man, from your Muskogee Nation, called on me several days ago, to collect taxes from me, same as if I was a merchant in the pursuit of selling merchandise to the people of your nation and others at Muskogee. I answered him that my line of business does not come under that clause as I am not selling goods at all, but only buy for cash the produce of the people of the Muskogee Nation such as Beef Hides, Wool, Deer Skins, Furs and Pecan Nuts, and these I ship to the States for Disposal...

I also told him that I would write to you in reference to this case for the proper explanation of your national law upon the same, and whatever your decision in a letter to me would be he and I would abide and conform to it, which was satisfactory to him.

That you may fully see into this case, it is proper for me to inform you that I own no buildings here, whether for business or residence purchased, as I and my family are boarding here and the warehouse is here...(Indecipherable name) was kind enough to give me partitioned space for my use without any compensation whatever. He is an old acquaintance of mine, knowing thoroughly my present embarrassed financial condition.

It is now 18 years that I bought...personally or through agents hides, furs, pecans, etc., etc. in the Muskogee Nation and have never been called upon to pay any tax until now for the mere privilege of buying your peoples' produce for Cash. When I came to your Nation in 1867 I was quite well off, and since then disbursed directly and indirectly in Cash over $20,000 for their produce in my line and never having sold them one Dollar's worth of merchandise...

Today I am a poor man having lost all I possessed in this business and the time of 13 years of the best and most active part of a man's life, between the age of 27 and 40. I am making now a new start in life on borrowed capital from my most intimate friends in St. Louis, Mo., whereas most Merchants who sold goods to your people in the last 13 years started with comparatively little and are now in Easy Circumstances and not a few are very well off. I have brought my Money, my Time and my Labor to your people but never took a Dollar out of your Country. I can without Egotism...assert that I have been a great benefit to the people of the Muskogee Nation and other Nations in Indian Territory.

The very nature and Cash Basis of my Business can not help but be of benefit to any producing country. Hence it would be in my humble opinion unjust, neither wise policy or good statesmanship to further the welfare and interest of your people by taxing men who bring money into your Country and who stimulate productions for the mere privilege of being permitted to buy their produce for Cash and not Barter in exchange for anything else but Cash. In my judgement, it is the undoubted interest of your people to encourage competition for men in my line to come to your Nation and buy their produce for Cash only and not discourage them by a 100 dollar tax on such a Business, which tax could have been only intended for merchants who sell them goods, which takes their money out of a country not in.

Of course if there exists a law on your Statute Books that men who buy produce even for Cash, notwithstanding they do not sell anything, are also subject to a certain tax—then I come under that clause; but if it does not say so, then in that instance I am not subject to any tax at all as the one applying to merchants selling goods could not reasonably have any reference to my business at all. You will oblige me to inform me at your very earliest convenience of your explanation and decision on this matter and whether I am subject to any tax—and if so, to what amount? so that I can show your letter to your tax collector when he calls on me again, your answer to me to be as an instruction to him in this or similar cases.

I have the honor to be your most obedient servant.
(Signed) Joseph Sondheimer[53]

Sondheimer's points appear to be well-taken. By purchasing produce from the Indians and not offering it for re-sale as a dealer, he became the classic middleman, a wholesaler. In addition, his goods were not offered to dealers within Indian Territory but rather were being shipped to the other states or out of the country. The Creek national law with regard to the trader's tax clearly applied to "dealers." Whether Checote, under whose administration the tax law was enacted, was aware of the distinctions between dealer and wholesaler is quite another matter. But as indicated in the letter that follows, Checote seemed to be aware of the distinctions but was simply not inclined to do anything about revising the statutes to accommodate Sondheimer. For at least the next twenty years, through the administrations of all of Checote's successors, the language of the statute remained the same—"on each dealer in hides, peltry, furs, wool, pecans and other country produce." The finer points relating to the functions of the different marketing intermediaries were paid no heed whatsoever. All that had changed between 1880 and 1900 was a reduction in the tax from $100 to $50.

Sondheimer's plea for relief based upon his "embarrassed financial condition" was most likely a familiar wail to the chief, and was disregarded.[54] So, too, was Sondheimer's claim about stimulating the economy. True as the claim may have been, those who start the fires of commerce, as Sondheimer undoubtedly did, then as now find their way to the top of the "light horseman's" list.[55]

Nearly a year after he wrote Checote, Sondheimer received an official response from the chief:

May 23, 1881

Joseph Sondheimer
Muskogee, Ind. Ty.

Dear Sir:

The matter relating to the payment of the "trading tax" by
you has been carefully considered, and it is now deemed
best that you be not excused from the payment of the same.
You will therefore remit it in the same manner as other
merchants doing business within the limits of the Nation.
But, if the matter is brought up during the next session of
our National Council, your claim for reduction will be
presented. The executive is aware of the peculiarities of
your position but any omission in favor of you would
furnish a precedent for non-enforcement of our laws in the
future.

Very respectfully
Princ. Chief, M.N.[56]

There was no one to whom Sondheimer could appeal. He
would pay his taxes. At stake was his trader's license, which was
subject to renewal each year. Annual renewals were issued by the
U.S. Indian agent but only after the agent had conferred with
Checote to find out if the trader in question had paid his taxes
and conducted himself honorably with the Indians in the previous year.

On March 5, 1881, just before Checote wrote Sondheimer,
the Indian agent had written Checote, informing him that two
German Jews, Elias and Harry Laupheimer,[57] who also traded in
hides and furs in Muskogee, along with 23 other traders,
including Sondheimer, had been granted licenses to trade with
the Creeks for another year. The letter carried this admonition:
"If any refuse to pay the tax required by Creek law, please inform
me."[58]

Sondheimer was not in Muskogee at the time Checote's letter
arrived, and it's fair to assume he left instructions with an

employee not to carry the fight further in case Checote turned down his plea. Sondheimer was an outspoken man, but he was also practical, and certainly he was no fool. He obviously reasoned that neither the tax bill nor the principle behind it was worth losing his trader's license over. The day following receipt of Checote's letter, a Sondheimer employee, one A.T. Hearn, wrote Checote, informing the chief that Sondheimer was away in Texas for two months and assuring him that "there should be no trouble getting your money when he comes back."[59]

Checote, in 1882, was selected by the Methodist Episcopal Church, South, as a delegate to the Ecumenical Conference in London, attended by delegates from various countries throughout the world. But the chief, who had fallen ill, was not able to attend. It perhaps had been the greatest honor bestowed upon him, the culmination of a lifetime of service to Methodism.[60] During the next few years, his health gradually worsened. Afflicted with Bright's disease, the chief was now nearing the end. His friends tried to raise $250 to send him to Hot Springs, Arkansas, but on September 13, 1884, he died at his humble farmhouse near Okmulgee before the money could be collected. He was sixty-five.[61] He left a wife and six children. His property consisted of a "few horses and some cattle, five apple trees, a vegetable garden, and a watch and chain worth $85."[62]

His most valuable legacy was his lifetime of service to his people and his God. Historian O.A. Lambert, who once served as president of the Creek Indian Memorial Association, wrote: "As we have talked to the 'old Indians' of today about Checote, they all speak of him as their 'Great Chief,' gentle as a child, courageous as a lion, whose life left an impress on his people for good more than all other chiefs in their history."[63]

Joseph Sondheimer, in the meantime, continued to prosper in Muskogee. *The Muskogee Evening Times* of September 16, 1901, carried a story noting that Sondheimer was appointed to a citizen's committee to make arrangements for a memorial service honoring President McKinley.[64] In 1904, he was offered the post of mayor of Muskogee, but declined.[65]

Muskogee had two major fires in its history, one in 1877, the other in 1899, the latter the most devastating of the two, the town being virtually destroyed. After the fire, Muskogee's leading citizens met at the Sondheimer hide house, which had withstood the conflagration, and set about planning a new Muskogee. It was Sondheimer himself who was leader of the group and the man instrumental in conceiving a new town layout.[66]

Long after his tax problem with Checote was resolved, the outspoken Sondheimer continued to register unhappiness about taxes. In 1906, the following interview with Sondheimer appeared in the *Muskogee Times-Democrat:*

> "I should not like to leave Muskogee," said Joseph Sondheimer sadly, as he sat in front of his famous hide house on Second Street this morning. "No," he continued, "I do not want to leave Muskogee, and yet, what can I do when everybody seems to be going crazy. I have always prided myself on my sanity. I am one of the oldest residents of Indian Territory, and while I have not done as much as some persons, I hope I am favorably known. Now I am surrounded by crazy men and I'm afraid I might go crazy, too...
>
> The tax assessor is crazy, for he has assessed property so high that nobody can live here. My neighbor, Mr. Scales, of Dallas, Texas, bought ninety-five feet of ground and paid $100 per foot for it. He started to put up a large building to cost $20,000 and the assessor raised the value to $350 per foot. This will drive away investors who want to improve the city...[67]

One of Sondheimer's greatest desires was for Oklahoma to achieve statehood, and he lived long enough to see it eventually happen in 1907. Four years earlier, he reminisced about his life in Indian Territory:

While I have prospered reasonably, yet I feel that I have wasted my life in coming so early and staying so long in this country. I have missed the pleasures and comforts to be found farther east, and now that I am old I realize it more keenly than ever. Year after year, we have waited for the gates of Indian Territory to become unlocked and the tribal walls to be broken down for the entrance of a better civilization only to be disappointed and then buoyed up by a new hope which faded away like its predecessors. I sympathize with the full-blood Indian in the change now taking place. He was a good man in the old days, honest and law-abiding. Hard times are in store for him.[68]

In expressing sympathy for the Indian over "the change now taking place," Sondheimer was more than likely referring to the work of the Dawes Commission. A few years earlier, the commission had patiently set about negotiating with the Five Tribes, seeking to make allotments of land to individual tribal members and to have their tribal governments abandoned.[69] At first, the Indians' response was openly hostile, but later their mood gradually began to change. They recognized that any further struggle would be fruitless. The insults to their tribal integrity had already gone too far.

The building of the "Katy" railroad through their domain over thirty years earlier was largely responsible for the Indians' present predicament. The railroad not only facilitated entry into their lands of the worst class of white adventurer and vagabond but in and of itself became a highly unprofitable venture for the railroad's bondholders. The railroads and their lobbyists in Washington, in order to pay off their bonded indebtedness, desperately needed access to more white settlements and to more white enterprises. They would not be denied.[70]

By the turn of the century, it was all over for the Indians. The land that had been theirs "so long as the grass grew and the rivers flowed" would be divided among the Indians in preparation for statehood. Each tribal member would have an equal share of the total land in Indian Territory. The total area of the five nations was 19,525,966 acres. Of this, the 18,712 enrolled members of the Creek tribe each received 160 acres from their tribal domain of approximately three million acres.[71]

On November 20, 1906, a constitution was adopted for the proposed state of Oklahoma which combined Indian Territory with Oklahoma Territory. It was ratified by a vote of the people and presented for signature to President Theodore Roosevelt. The president proclaimed Oklahoma a state on November 16, 1907.[72]

That vast expanse of land west of the Mississippi soon would pass almost totally to the white man. Two men who never aroused the interest of the historians, one a Jewish immigrant, the other a Creek Indian chief, nevertheless played their own special, symbolically important roles, in the absurdities, the sadness and the bitterness of that transition.

Joseph Sondheimer, last of the great fur traders, died July 10, 1913, his dream of statehood realized. The remains of this rugged and outspoken pioneer rest today alongside his estranged wife and his son, Samuel, at Mount Sinai cemetery in St. Louis, close to the old chapel, a mere 75 feet away from the fast lanes of Gravois Avenue.[73]

Samuel Checote, who died a generation earlier, lies buried behind the Newtown Methodist Church, outside the little town of Okmulgee, the capitol of the Creek nation. His unmarked grave site has been obscured by a century-old growth of weeds and underbrush, and is indistinguishable to the observer. The great Creek chief died without knowing that the dream he had for his people would never be realized.

In response to a query in 1937, Orlando Swain, secretary of the Creek Indian Memorial Association, noted sadly that Checote's "grave has been very much neglected much to our disgrace."[74]

Chapter 6

THE STRANGE CASE OF DON SOLOMONO

On a cold, windswept morning in May, 1885, a wedding took place at the Acoma pueblo in New Mexico Territory. The entire village turned out for the ceremony, the Indians crowding into the old church whose ten-foot thick adobe walls reached over sixty-feet high to a heavy, timbered ceiling. The mission, which was built in the seventeenth century, was named for Saint Estevan, the first martyr and patron saint of the Acoma Indians, and had served as a fortress for the embattled tribe during the pueblo revolts of 1680.

The bride was a young Indian girl named Juana Valle, the granddaughter of the governor of the pueblo, Martin Valle. She spoke no English, only Spanish and Queres, the native tongue of the tribe. The groom was a small, portly white man in his middle thirties. He was Solomon Bibo, formerly of Brakel, Westphalia, Germany, the son of Cantor Isaac Bibo.[1] The Indians called him Don Solomono. He had been in the New Mexico Territory for more than seventeen years. His command of English was poor but he spoke Spanish and Queres fluently. It was no easy task for a white man to learn the Indians' tongue,[2] but this affable Indian trader had spent many years at the pueblo and had a quick, adaptive mind.

The wedding was remarkable in many ways. The Indians were Roman Catholics, having been converted to the faith in 1628 by the Spaniards. However, they still held fast to their ancient tribal beliefs and rituals. Solomon Bibo was a Jew, and while he lived among the Indians and was on this day married out of the sight of his God, he, too, held fast to his religious heritage. All the more unusual was the fact that the Indians had an intense dislike for white men, dating back to their disputes over their aboriginal land grants. Yet here, standing with his bride in the thick red-brown dust of the mission floor, was Solomon Bibo, not only a white man, but a Jew, and while there was distrust for most white men there was only love by the Indians for this Jewish immigrant.

The Acoma pueblo, sitting high on a mesa, is located thirteen miles south of Interstate 40 on state route 13, about sixty miles west of Albuquerque. In this part of the state, the elevation is deceptively high, some 7,000 feet above the sea. Yet there is the illusion of being in a basin because the land is flat and the mountain ranges in the distance form a rim around the area. The unbroken flatness of the land is interrupted only by stunning blue-brown mesas rising sharply from the high desert, and here and there by grotesquely shaped rock formations.

They call the Acoma pueblo Sky City because it rises 360 feet above the desert under a big New Mexico sky. But to the Indians who have resided here for centuries and still speak the Queresan language, the city high on the rock is called by its nickname, Ako—in Queresan, "a place that always was."[3] It is today, in fact, the oldest continuously settled community in the United States, dating back, some archaeologists say, to before the birth of Christ.

The Acoma reservation today is home for one of the nineteen different pueblo tribes in New Mexico and is made up of three parts— Acoma, the old village on top of the mesa; Acomita, a farm community located in the north valley of the reservation; and McCarty's, located on the reservation's north gap, along the right of way of the Atchison, Topeka and Santa Fe railroad.[4]

Three miles north of Acoma, rising sharply higher and steeper than Sky City, is Katzimo, the Enchanted Mesa. There is a story that Katzimo was once inhabited, but that one day a severe storm destroyed the rock trail leading to the settlement on top; and unable to descend to the valley for food, the natives eventually died of hunger.[5] It still remains a mystery whether anyone had lived on Katzimo, but as legend has it, "no one ever climbs that mesa, for the pathway down will vanish behind them."[6]

The primary language of the Indians is Queresan, and most also speak English. Only a few elders still speak Spanish. It was not always that way. Solomon Bibo had little opportunity to improve his English while operating his trading post at the pueblo. Queresan and Spanish were then the primary and secondary tongues, and to have heard English spoken was a rarity.[7]

The reservation today consists of 245,672 acres in contrast to the 94,196 acres of the original Spanish land grant patented by the United States in 1877. The present lands were set aside by Congress in March, 1928, after recognizing the pueblo's need for additional pasture land. Solomon Bibo, who several decades earlier, helped the Indians petition for surveys to increase their boundaries, lived long enough to see his hopes for the Indians fulfilled.

For four centuries the Indians of Acoma have lived under the domination of three different nations—Spain, Mexico and the United States. During that time there has been a continuous and complex problem arising from the lands originally granted to the various New Mexico pueblos by the Spaniards. The troubled years have been marked by an endless stream of disputes between the Indians and the nations in power, between the Indians and the white settlers, and even among the pueblos themselves. From 1684, when the Spaniards first made their land grants to the Indians until this very day, the disputes, in one form or another, still remain unresolved. That is why a recounting of any tale played out in the history of New Mexico—no matter how important or how trivial—will in some way be rooted in the unending controversy over land ownership. And so it is too with the strange case of Solomon Bibo.

Shortly before his wedding to Juana Valle, Bibo was charged October 1, 1884, in the district court, second judicial district, territory of New Mexico, with defrauding the Indians of their land. Although the case was adjudicated long ago, Bibo's guilt or innocence is still open to question to this day.

In order to get a better understanding of the Bibo case, we must return to a time long before Bibo came to the Acoma pueblo, back to the time when the Spanish first discovered the city on the rock.

The first historical reference to Acoma came in 1539. Fray Marcos de Niza, returning from an expedition to Mexico, told of a settlement on the mesa, referring to it as a Kingdom of Hacus. Hearing of the discovery, Francisco Coronado, the Spanish explorer, dispatched Captain Hernando Alvarado to explore further. The following year, Alvarado had reached the pueblo, describing it as "a very strange place built upon a solid rock." Alvarado's men, after climbing the rock trail to the summit of the mesa, were greeted by the Indians and made welcome. They were presented with gifts of food, for there was no hint of aggression by Alvarado's men. It was merely a routine exploration, and as a consequence the Indians, unthreatened, were friendly to their visitors. At this time the population of the pueblo was 200.

Because of its location high on the mesa, Acoma is a natural fortress, difficult for any enemy to penetrate. The rock trail to the top, then as now, is nearly perpendicular at various points, and scaling the summit would be a precarious task were it not for the indentations in the rocks—literally finger and toe holes—scratched out of the rock from centuries of clawing and clutching by the Indians.

Subsequent Spanish expeditions came to the pueblo in 1581 and 1582, without consequence. But in 1598, Spain believed it was necessary to force submission of the Indians, so the following year Vincente de Zaldivar and a force of seventy men stealthily scaled the rock trail to the top of the mesa, and after a fierce struggle managed to overpower the Indians and take command of the village, despite being greatly outnumbered. Save for occasional abortive insurgencies by the natives, the pueblo remained under Spanish domination until 1680. At that time the Spaniards made the mistake of trying to prohibit the Indians' tribal worship practices, and as a result were overthrown in the great pueblo revolt.

Fifty years earlier, in 1629, a gentle Franciscan, Fray Juan Ramirez, had arrived at the pueblo. He had been forewarned that the Indians were bitterly hostile toward white men, but the intrepid Franciscan won the Indians over, taught them to read and write, led them to Christianity, and built the mission San Estevan. Christianity somehow managed to co-exist with the Indians' tribal practices until the Spanish, in their religious zeal, pressed for monolithic worship.

After the pueblo revolt, Acoma remained independent until the Spanish reconquered the pueblo in 1692. Spanish domination continued for the next 130 years until the signing of the Treaty of Cordova in 1821, when New Spain became New Mexico, part of the Mexican nation.

Historians have often given the impression that the Indians were oppressed under the Spaniards. Actually, the opposite was true. The conquerors were far more humane to the conquered than they were given credit for. Historian-archaeologist, Charles F. Lummis, a friend of Solomon and Juana, pointed out that there were seventy-six pueblos at the time of Spain's conquest of the Indians, but through the efforts of the Spaniards, the Indians were persuaded to concentrate into far fewer pueblos, thus insuring greater safety from predatory neighbors. These pueblo concentrations became the Spanish land grants, which are still at issue today. In 1893, Lummis described the effect of Spanish rule on the Indians:

> The most important effect of the coming of Spain was to
> make the pueblo from a sedentary to a fixed Indian...To
> each of his communities was given a generous grant of
> land, and upon that grant he must stay. Thenceforth there
> were no town migrations, and the living pueblos are
> essentially where they were when Plymouth Rock came into

history...With greater fixity of abode he has still further increased the distance between himself and the nomad. His perceptions have grown less acute than those of the hunted hunter— though still far ahead of the Caucasian—but he has reflected more, acquired more, and preserved more. His traditions have accumulated to a huge mass; his laws are well-formulated; his internal religion has been bewilderingly complex. It is fortunate for archaeology that the Spaniard was his brother's keeper. Had the pueblo enjoyed sixteenth century acquaintance with the Saxons, we should be limited now to unearthing and articulating his bones.[8]

It has been well over a century since Solomon Bibo first came to the pueblo. What he saw when he first arrived was almost the same as what Alvarado had seen in 1540, the only exception being the mission San Estevan and the adjoining cemetery. The adobe houses were almost exactly the same. Built on the surface of the rock, they were three stories high and lined up in three parallel rows, running east and west and facing south. The houses were constructed similarly; all were private and con-nected, with the top floor used for the living room, the middle floor for sleeping and the ground floor for storage. The first story of the houses had no doorways. To gain entrance, the Indians used an outside ladder which led directly to the balcony of the second floor.

Bibo, whose trading post was located near the mission at the south edge of the rock, drew his trade from a population of approximately 435 people, or 124 families,[9] about twice the inhabitants as when Acoma was first discovered by the Span-iards.

Today, as in the past, Acoma land is used for grazing, but farming is the chief occupation, wheat, beans, corn, alfalfa and chili being the main produce.

Acoma has strongly resisted moving into the twentieth cen-tury. The older tribal members, in order to hold their power, have tried to keep the pueblo essentially the same as it was in former centuries.[10] The *cacique* (the chief), the medicine men, the war chief and the governor, part of the same tribal hierarchy of the past, still remain in control. The Queres tongue is still spoken. As late as the early 1930s, in fact, very few of the older residents had ventured more than a few miles from the reservation, and about ninety-nine percent of the tribe still continues to reside on Acoma lands.

The old village on the mesa is now only a symbolic home for the tribe, and no longer the main village. The Indians, for the most part, live in the valley surrounding the mesa, although a few keep their residence in the old village during the warmer months of the year.

The income of the Indians remains pitifully low. Those who aren't engaged in farming, work at various types of employment off the reservation. Certain essential services like gas stations, restaurants, motels and other service facilities are not found on the reservation. The Indians take care of their shopping needs in small Mexican-American communities nearby.[11]

With this background on Acoma in place, we can return to the Bibo story. Solomon Bibo was born August 29, 1853 in Prussia, the sixth of eleven children of Blumchen Rosenstein Bibo and Isaac Bibo. He emigrated to America in 1869 when he was sixteen, leaving his homeland for the usual reasons: the intensification of anti-semitism in Germany as well as the promise of greater economic opportunity in America. Beyond these factors, however, Bibo was influenced by the tales of his maternal grandfather, Lucas Rosenstein, who had come to America in 1812 to escape conscription in Napoleon's army. Lucas stayed in America for twelve years but returned to Prussia to marry his childhood sweetheart. The old man had vivid recollections of America, and his tales had a strong effect not only on young Solomon but on his brothers, Nathan, Emil and Simon.

Nathan and Simon, the first two Bibo brothers to come to America, are believed to have spent very little time on the eastern seaboard when they arrived in 1866. As adventuresome young men, they headed straight for New Mexico where, being part of the German-Jewish network, they worked for a time for the Spiegelberg brothers' mercantile business in Santa Fe. At this time, Santa Fe was a hotbed of commerce. There were plenty of dry goods' firms, which meant too much competition; and furthermore the two entrepreneurial brothers wanted no part of steady employment with the Staab or Spiegelberg families, the pioneer German-Jewish merchant clans of Santa Fe. Instead they pushed farther westward toward Albuquerque. Eventually, Simon and Nathan opened a trading post at the small village of Ceboletta, New Mexico, trading with the Navajos. When Solomon arrived three years later, he spent a somewhat longer time on the eastern seaboard than his brothers, primarily to get some familiarity with the English language. But in due course he moved westward and joined his brothers in partnership in Ceboletta.[12]

History has not fully accounted for the activities of the Bibos in the late 1870s, but it was known that, circa 1871, Simon was a licensed trader for a time at the Laguna pueblo, a sister pueblo to Acoma.[13] In addition, both Bibo brothers, for a time, were engaged in bidding on the produce requirements for Fort Wingate and Fort Defiance, with the Indians as their primary produce suppliers. Emil Bibo was also an Indian trader; however, the circumstances surrounding Emil's business relationship with his brothers is not clearly documented; although all four brothers, apart from their skills as traders, shared one virtue in common: they were all friends and supporters of the Indians and closely involved in the Indians' land boundary problems.

Solomon eventually arrived at Acoma in 1882, setting up his trading post near the mission. But from the outset, he had difficulties with the U.S. Indian Service in obtaining a trader's license. It is conjectured that because Solomon, even before arriving at Acoma, was an outspoken advocate of securing more land for the Indians, at the expense of the Mexicans, he found himself mired in political quicksand. He was considered a trouble-maker by the Mexicans, who believed that the Indians were trying to dispossess them from their property in an effort to reclaim their aboriginal lands. Not only was Bibo regarded by the Mexicans as being clearly partisan to the Indians, but in addition he was regarded as "un rico Israelito," a rich Jew.[14] It is speculated that Bibo, in finally securing his trader's license, had received help from the Spiegelberg clan whose influence in territorial politics as well as in the drawing rooms of Santa Fe was considerable. The German Jews in the West were indeed quick to come to the aid of one of their own.

In April, 1884, a year prior to his marriage to Juana, the Acoma tribe, in an action that to this day defies explication, leased its entire 94,196 acres to Solomon Bibo. Nothing in life was as important to the tribe as its land, yet for a period of thirty years the Indians signed away the rights to their precious patent to Bibo, the full land title which was officially granted to them in 1877.

The lease called for Bibo to pay the tribe $300 per year for the first ten years; $400 per year for the second ten years; and $500 per year for the remaining ten years—in all, $12,000 for the full thirty years. Bibo in return would be responsible for protecting the Indians' cattle and for keeping squatters off the land. However, under the provisions of the lease, Bibo had both water and mining rights to the patent, and would pay the Indians ten cents per ton for each ton of coal taken from the land. A further provision of the lease was that Bibo had the right to assign it to any other party at any time during the life of the contract.[15]

Martin Valle, grandfather of Bibo's future bride, was governor of the pueblo at the time the lease was drawn. Valle could neither read nor write, but as governor was empowered to act for the pueblo in business matters, as long as the matters represented the will of the entire pueblo. Valle indicated his approval on the lease with his mark.[16]

Not long after the lease was signed, Bibo assigned the lease to Joseph E. Saint and A. W. Cleland doing business as Saint and Cleland Cattle Co. The firm held the lease for several years but eventually went out of business. The lease then reverted to Bibo who held it until it terminated.[17]

On the same day that Bibo assigned his lease to Saint and

Cleland, he also sold the firm two parcels of land he owned adjacent to the Acoma grant. He was paid $16,000 for the property. At the same time, Solomon's brother, Nathan, sold another piece of land to Saint and Cleland for $1,000.[18] The cattle company, not surprisingly, was named in the suit against Bibo.

The true significance of the Indians' lease to Bibo can best be understood by recounting how the lands were granted to the Indians originally. Only in this way can the full magnitude of the Indians' benevolence to the immigrant be adequately measured.

The Spanish made their grants to eleven pueblos in 1689. The pueblos were Acoma, Jimez, San Juan, Pecuries, San Felipe, Pecos, Cochita, Santa Domingo, Zia, Zuni and Laguna. The Spaniards realized the Indians, as crown vassals, would need land to live on and cultivate.[19]

The Spaniards allocated land by measuring a specified number of leagues outward in each of the four cardinal directions from the center of the pueblos. In this way, each pueblo's grant was fixed.

As crown vassals, the Indians had all the privileges of any Spaniard. They were entitled to their own lands and to full protection by both church and civil authorities. Non-Indians were strictly forbidden to reside on Indian property, much less stop for the night if any other facilities were available. The Indians' rights to their lands were inviolate. They had to live in their own pueblos and were forbidden to take up residence in another village.[20] Moreover, they were not allowed to buy or sell their property without the approval of the Spanish authorities, a matter which would later be central to the Bibo case. All that Spain asked in return from the Indians was that they become Christians, that they marry under Christian law and that they learn to speak Spanish.[21]

Of all rights and privileges accorded to the Indians under Spanish rule none turned out to be as important as prior water rights to all streams and rivers and other water which crossed or bordered their lands. It is this specific regulation by the Spanish crown which has become the fundamental basis for the present day three-way legal dispute among the pueblo Indians, the descendants of the Spanish settlers and New Mexico's growing, affluent Anglo population.

When on September 16, 1821, Mexico won her independence from Spain, the Mexicans were bound by treaty to uphold Spanish laws with regard to Indian land policy. Although the Indians were wards of the government under Spanish rule, the Mexicans nevertheless gave them the title of citizens. And as citizens, they were able to sell, trade or otherwise change their land grants, something they were prevented from doing under Spanish rule.

Historian Herbert O. Brayer raised this question:

> While there is no question that the acts of the Mexican people did confer citizenship on the Indians, there is serious doubt as to just what is meant by citizenship...Are infants, children, idiots, lunatics and spendthrifts not citizens?[22]

Spanish law, which the Mexicans were treaty bound to up-hold, stated that non-Indians could not arbitrarily get control of pueblo lands, and theoretically this was enforced. On a practical level, however, it was not enforced. Mexican administrators and officials, by falsifying titles to lands granted by Spain to the Indians, were able to alienate pueblo lands without the Indians knowing it. In addition, white squatters invaded the Indians' lands, and the Indians, without protection, gradually saw their land holdings diminish.

The change from Mexican to U.S. rule, twenty-five years later, in 1846, had confusing ramifications for the pueblos. One outgrowth of the transition was that Solomon Bibo, or anyone else, whether on a fair or unfair basis, could make any deal at all with the Indians, including one for their land.

In order to cast additional light on the Bibo case, it would be helpful to outline briefly U.S. policies toward the pueblos in those paradoxical years after the acquisition of New Mexico.

At that time, in 1846, the pueblo Indians automatically became full-fledged U.S. citizens and immediately the U.S. was confronted with two problems it would search long and hard for the answers to. One problem was how to deal with the erosion of Indian lands by non-Indians which had occurred under Mexico. The other was how to justify the restraints the U.S. wanted to impose on the Indians without depriving them of their rights as citizens, rights they were accorded under the provisions of the Treaty of Guadalupe Hidalgo in 1848.

Under section six of the treaty, the United States had to recognize the rights of Mexican citizens with respect to property and other civil matters. Because the Mexicans had declared the Indians citizens when New Spain became New Mexico in 1821, the U.S. was now forced to accord the Indians the same status. As a result the pueblo Indians occupied a unique position, one entirely different from their brethren living on various western reservations. Indians on other lands, subject to the Non-Intercourse Act of 1834, fell under the jurisdiction of the Bureau of Indian Affairs, with no rights, therefore, to alienate their lands, rights the pueblo Indians now had.[23] In short, U.S. policy toward Indians was split. The U.S. long before had considered Indians wards of the government, believing they were savages who required the severest of restraints.

In 1876, nearly 30 years after the Treaty of Guadalupe Hidalgo, the Supreme Court, in *U.S. v. Joseph,* fortified the provisions of the treaty, holding that the pueblo Indians were, in effect, not Indians at all, and therefore the laws of the land with respect to other Indians did not apply to them. For that reason, they had complete title to their lands and could dispose of them as they saw fit.[24]

Furthermore, the pueblos were assured that their land grants under Spain would hold safe. For this reason, in 1854, the Office of Surveyor General was established to investigate land ownership claims and determine their validity. It was important that the aboriginal land claims of the pueblos be decided once and for all. Even while the New Mexico Territory had been under

U.S. jurisdiction, there had been further encroachments on pueblo lands by recently arrived white squatters. In addition, there had been recurring boundary disputes between the Acoma and Laguna pueblos, fueled in part by Mexican officials to serve their own interests. So a clear delineation of boundary lines became essential. The Surveyor General's office had its hands full.[25]

The Laguna and Acoma pueblos co-exist harmoniously today, but through most of the eighteenth century the two pueblos were continually embroiled in boundary squabbles. Bibo, understandably, was always a defender of Acoma in the disputes. This did not endear him to the neighboring pueblo, to the white traders at Laguna or to the Mexicans whose interests were better served with Laguna.

Acoma was beset by problems, and there was no way the Bureau of Indian Affairs could intercede. Had the tribe been under U.S. jurisdiction in 1834, when the Indian Non-Intercourse Act was enacted, they would have had automatic protection from all land encroachments.[26] At this time, however, their only recourse was through the courts, and such an action it would seem was simply too difficult and confusing for the Indians to take on their own initiative.

In 1858, a survey of Acoma lands was undertaken by the surveyor's office. The Indians could offer little proof of their aboriginal land boundaries. There were no maps, no boundary stakes. As a result the outcome was unfavorable, but still no official patent was issued.[27] Additional surveys were made in 1876 and 1877, but these too were unfavorable for Acoma.

In 1877, President Rutherford B. Hayes confirmed the survey of 1858 and Acoma received its patent of 94,196 acres, a patent which the Indians found inadequate, for it was far from what they believed they were entitled to. Bibo continued to petition the government for further land surveys after the patent was granted. No matter how he tried, Bibo could not help the tribe; and even though their case was not proved, the Indians never forgot Bibo's efforts to restore their aboriginal lands.

Shortly after Bibo entered into his agreement with the Indians, Pedro Sanchez, the Indian agent based in Santa Fe, found out about the lease, and on June 4, 1884, two months after the lease was signed, wrote an angry letter to Hiram Price, Commissioner of Indian Affairs. He told Price that Bibo had taken advantage of the Indians, and that it was outrageous of Bibo, on seeing the "blindness" of the Indians, to make them "prey to (his) sagacity." [28] Sanchez, in alleging the lease was obtained through pressure, also contended that the mark of Martin Valle on the lease only expressed the will of Martin Valle, and not of the pueblo in common.

Price's response to Sanchez was that his office would not condone Bibo's action. He then instructed Sanchez to determine if the lease was indeed the will of the pueblo, and if not then to notify Bibo to surrender the lease or else forfeit his trader's license. [29] It would appear that Price and Sanchez had made up their minds that Bibo had deliberately defrauded the Indians, for the terms of the lease as well as its immediate reassignment to Saint and Cleland were, on the surface, so outrageously in Bibo's favor, to the detriment of the pueblo, that it would be difficult for them to conclude otherwise.

From a legal standpoint, Price and Sanchez realized that, despite whatever objections they might have to the lease on any other grounds, it would be valid if it were obtained with the consent of the pueblo in common. The *cacique* and the *principales* in the tribal hierarchy would also have to have given their consent, not Martin Valle alone. [30]

Sanchez met with Valle, and handed him an affidavit to sign which in essence stated that Bibo had led Valle to believe the lease was for three years, not thirty years, and that even for the reduced time period, Valle unintentionally had given Bibo mining rights to the Indians' land. Valle then made his mark on the affidavit. [31] With Valle's testimony in his pocket, Sanchez met with 60 members of the tribe at McCarty's, and asked if they had consented to the Bibo lease. All quickly denied that they had given their consent, Martin Valle included. Valle, in fact, repeated what he had sworn to in the affidavit.

Sanchez now had the documentation he needed to have

Bibo's license rescinded, a recommendation which he passed forward to Commissioner Price. Bibo, in the meantime, had a confrontation with Sanchez, and maintained to the Indian agent that the lease was legally binding, and that he had no intention of setting it aside. When he was apprised of Bibo's position, Price instructed Sanchez immediately to revoke Bibo's trader's license.[32]

Shortly after Sanchez's meeting at McCarty's, the Indians, childlike and malleable, petitioned the commissioner to permit Bibo's license to continue in force. The Acoma tribe was so afraid it would lose the love and friendship of Solomon Bibo that it produced 100 signatures asking that Bibo's license not be revoked.

The Indians' petition was a result of the efforts of Solomon's brother, Simon.[33] Simon believed that no one could prevent Solomon from trading with the Indians as long as the Indians wanted him. "His intentions with the Indians," Simon had written, "are of the best nature and beneficial to them — because the men, women and children love him as they would love a father and he is in the same manner attached to them."[34]

It was Simon's contention that two traders at the Laguna pueblo, Walter and Robert Marmon, as well as Agent Sanchez himself, had conspired to discredit Bibo and have the lease set aside.[35] Simon sought the help of General Whittlesey, a member of the Board of Indian Commissioners. He reported to Whittlesey that the Marmons had originally attempted to lease Acoma lands themselves, and had offered the Indians one cow a year for ten years. The Indians, having full trust in Solomon Bibo, approached him for counsel on the Marmon proposal, and were told that the terms were inadequate. At this point, Solomon offered to lease the land himself. It was clear that if Solomon hadn't responded with his own offer, the Indians would have struck a deal with the Marmons, one that would have been far less favorable than Bibo's own offer.[36]

Simon's story had impressed Whittlesey, and he was now convinced that Solomon's offer was made to stop the bad offer of the Marmons. Whittlesey then notified Price that he believed Bibo was truly a friend of the Indians and that the revocation of Bibo's trading license was not in the best interests of the tribe.[37]

Joseph Bell, the United States attorney, concluded in 1888, four years after the government brought suit against Bibo for defrauding the Indians of their land, that the government had no case. The Acoma Indians did not want to support the complaint. They did not want to turn their backs on their beloved friend. Since there were no complaints from the Indians, the court concluded that the charges against Bibo had no validity.

Pedro Sanchez was replaced as the Indian agent. The new agent, W. D. Williams, sent a letter to the pueblo in October, 1888. He wrote:

> To the people of the pueblo of Acoma, having confidence in the ability, integrity and fidelity of Solomon Bibo, and by virtue of the authority vested in me as Indian Agent by the United States, I hereby appoint Solomon Bibo, Governor of said pueblo, to take the place of Napoleon Pancho, the former Governor, and I also appoint the said Napoleon, Lieutenant Governor, and Yanie, Assistant Lieutenant Governor, to take the place of Manuel Concho, who is dismissed by my order, and I also appoint Jamie Sanchez Kasique, in place of Antonio, dismissed.
>
> (Signed) W.D. Williams
> U.S. Indian Agent[38]

Thus, Solomon Bibo, a Jewish immigrant, who four years earlier had been charged with defrauding the Indians of their land, was now governor of the pueblo, not just the only Jew but the only white man in the history of Acoma to hold that title, a title in the hierarchy of the tribe that carries the status of chief.

The strange case of Solomon Bibo will probably never be fully understood. He was a man, on one hand, who had a deep and genuine feeling for the Indians, who lived with them, spoke their language, even married into the tribe. He not only tried to help the Indians in their land disputes but also fought to improve the quality of their education. He helped, for example, to arrange for the admission of some of the Indians to the Carlisle Indian School, his own wife, Juana, included. But, on the other hand, Bibo was a man who apparently indulged in some questionable practices with the very people whose welfare so concerned him. How does one explain such contradictory behavior?

Perhaps, as an entrepreneur and trader, Bibo had an inbred need to make a good deal, and so made it. But this action, even if it was as unethical as it appeared to be, did not attenuate the inherent goodness of the man, whose regard for the Indians went far beyond mercenary considerations. Historian Frank McNitt wrote that "Solomon's interest in the Acoma's welfare — which in other matters may have been sincere — soon manifested itself."[39] The implication is clear. In contrast, Rabbi Floyd Fierman, a chronicler of Jews of the old West, concluded that the Indians, dating back to their rule under the Spaniards, were in constant fear that they might have their land taken away from them, and therefore couldn't be talked into doing what they really didn't want to do.[40]

In correspondence with Fierman, Arthur Bibo, a nephew of Solomon, wrote:

> At the National Archives I had access to a file in the Indian Department relative to the investigation about the thirty-year lease my Uncle Solomon executed with the tribe...the material tends to show that Uncle did something unethical or illegal. One must know all sides of the story to understand what really took place, and as I am familiar with the main facts I would advise you not to draw too hasty conclusions.[41]

And so conjecture continues, but the case remains a puzzle. What is far more palpable is that the policies and conduct of the United States toward the Indians has been, in all aspects, insensitive and unfair. The hapless Indian was legitimate prey for every trader pulling his wagon along the ruts of the Santa Fe trail. Yet through circumstances of acquisition and treaty, the pueblo Indians, whose culture was totally alien to the white man's, were citizens from 1848 to 1913, having no special governmental protection.

Finally, in 1913, the Bibo case became an academic matter. The Supreme Court, in the Sandoval decision, overturned the 1876 ruling in *U.S. v. Joseph* and held that the pueblo Indians were no longer citizens but wards of the government; and as a result all lands purchased from the Indians were invalid. In its decision, the court held the following:

> The people of the pueblos, although sedentary rather than
> nomadic in their inclinations and disposed to peace and
> industry, are nevertheless Indians in race, customs and
> domestic government...adhering to primitive modes of life,
> largely influenced by superstition and fetishism...They are
> essentially a simple, uninformed and inferior people.[42]

Solomon and Juana and their family moved to San Francisco in 1898. Solomon invested in real estate and was president of Bibo, Newman and Ikenberg, a fancy food store located at the corner of Polk and California streets. The business was destroyed in the earthquake of 1906. The move to California was largely prompted by Solomon's desire to give his children a Jewish education.

There were six Bibo children, four daughters and two sons.[43] The eldest boy, LeRoy, was bar mitzvah at Ohabai Shalome (the Bush Street synagogue). The younger son, Carl, attended religious school at Temple Emanuel, but was never bar mitzvah. Juana Bibo also observed the Jewish faith.[44]

Don Solomono, loved by the Indians as few white men ever were, died in San Francisco in 1934 at eighty-one. LeRoy and Carl Bibo said *kaddish* for their father at Congregation Shearith Israel. Juana Bibo died seven years later, in 1941. The Jewish Indian chief and his princess are buried in Colma, California, at the Home of Peace Mausoleum.

Their friend, Charles F. Lummis, had dedicated one of his books to Solomon and Juana. A typewritten copy of the dedication was sent to this writer in 1983 by Carl Bibo, the surviving son. The typed dedication read:

> To Sol and Juana Bibo, whom I have known and loved for forty years, since the dear old days in New Mexico, when they were beginning that married life which has been, to this day, so beautiful an example and so rare an inspiration. Dona Juana, of the oldest aristocracy in this country, worthy daughter of the First Americans, whose noble grandfather first told me the story of the Enchanted Mesa, is a much finer type than the storied Pocahontas, and of better blood. Don Solomon has left his mark all across New Mexico as one of the wisest, shrewdest, high-minded, most just and most generous of men that ever dealt with the natives of the Southwest. I write here of many things that they have shared, and I hope this book may bring back to them as many gentle memories as it does to me.[45]

On the typed copy of the dedication, the word "shrewdest" had been crossed out in ink.

Chapter 7

THE MAN WHO PAINTED INDIANS

It was the winter of 1853. A man sat huddled in his buffalo robes in the mountains of eastern Utah, trying to ward off the sub-zero cold and the hard, wind-driven snow.

He would soon have to leave the snowbank which afforded him his only protection from the elements and begin rounding up the horses which had strayed a mile deeper into the mountains. As he trudged after the horses, in the knee-deep snow, he found himself thinking of his mother and how, as a boy in Charleston, South Carolina, he had heard her response to his plea, one inclement night, to go outdoors and play: "I would not allow a cat to go out in such weather," his mother had said, "much less my son."

Surveying his surroundings, he wrote in his diary, "Dear Soul! How her heart would have ached for me if she had known a hundredth part of my sufferings."[1]

The wilderness of eastern Utah in the dead of winter was a most unlikely place to find Solomon Nunes Carvalho. He was a handsome man, still in his thirties, with long flowing hair. He was something of a momma's boy, fastidious to a fault and accustomed to the luxuries that were part of his heritage as a Jewish grandee. Highly educated and fluent in Latin and Greek, he carried himself with the elegance and dash of an aristocrat. Yet now he found himself with ten Delaware Indians and several treacherous muleskinners as companions. Were it not for Colonel John Charles Fremont, his leader, and Fremont's cadre of officers—Egloffstein, Fuller and Strobel—he would have found the Fremont expedition over the Rockies intolerable.[2]

Carvalho's participation in the Fremont expedition had begun one hot August afternoon in 1853. Fremont had come to Charleston to invite Carvalho to accompany him as official artist and daguerreotypist for his fifth expedition, an exploratory mission across the Rocky Mountains which would seek a transcontinental railroad route that would be serviceable all year 'round. Carvalho had jumped at the offer.

But now, in the cold wilderness of Utah, Carvalho, thinking about that August afternoon, wished he had said no. "I should have replied," he wrote in his diary, that "there were no inducements sufficiently powerful to have tempted me." But he had accepted Fremont's offer impulsively, not even stopping to consult with his family, so delighted was the artist at being asked by Fremont, a national hero, to accompany him. It had made no difference at the time that the exploration party would cross fearsome terrain which up until then had been seen by but a handful of white men, in a region where the winter weather was almost always brutal. But he had high regard for Fremont. "I know of no other man," Carvalho wrote, "to whom I would have trusted my life under similar circumstances."[3]

These details and countless others are carefully chronicled in Carvalho's book, *Incidents of Travel and Adventure in the Far West with Colonel Fremont's Last Expedition,* a jubilant, robust, sometime heart-rending account of Carvalho's experiences with the Fremont expedition.

Solomon Carvalho was a man of accomplishment and talent. He was, above all things, an artist, one of the first Jews in America to earn his living in that profession. His portraits of some of the great leaders of his age—Lincoln, Brigham Young, Fremont, and Walkara, the Ute Indian chief—are regarded today as invaluable works of art. He was also a skilled daguerreotypist, a master of photography, who had been taught by the pioneer of the art, Samuel F. B. Morse himself. In addition, Carvalho was a teacher, an inventor, an adventurer, a writer, a prayer book salesman, as well as a deeply religious Jew who was instrumental in the founding of the first Portuguese synagogue in Baltimore. As a man, he was a flamboyant dandy, greatly taken with himself, and a seeker after famous personages. However, this man of Jewish nobility, whose ancestors could be traced back to the time of the Spanish Inquisition, was, at bedrock, a resourceful, courageous and tough-minded Jew whose unlikely destiny it was to undergo some astonishing experiences among the Indians in his travels through the Rockies with Fremont.

John Charles Fremont had crossed and re-crossed great expanses of the Trans-Mississippi West in five expeditions between 1842 and 1853. He had followed trails to Oregon and California that had been carved out only by Indians and mountain men. His reports and maps cleared the way for settlers to move westward with some measure of assurance. He delineated trails, established the best times and methods for travel, and pinpointed the location of waterholes and grass for livestock grazing. Fremont, in short, was an advance man for the great western migrations. As his wife, Jessie Benton Fremont, put it: "From the ashes of his campfires have sprung cities."[4]

Despite all his enterprise, Fremont was unable to get government sanction for his fifth expedition, and had to finance it himself. His first three expeditions had been enormously successful, and he had been hailed as a national hero. His fourth expedition, however, was disastrous. He lost thirteen of his thirty-three men, and there were rumors that one of the thirteen had been killed and eaten by his comrades.[5] The failure of the fourth expedition was, to some extent, responsible for his being denied government support for the fifth expedition. But a larger factor in that failure was the opposition of Jefferson Davis, Secretary of War under President Pierce and the man responsible for such appointments. No other two men were more at odds, politically and philosophically, than Fremont and Davis. There was scarcely a matter on which they could agree. Davis was, of course, pro-slavery, Fremont an abolitionist, and their opposing view on this matter was the main reason why Fremont did not receive official sponsorship of the expedition.[6]

Two expeditions were already in the field when Fremont's began. All three were seeking the optimum railroad route through the Rockies. One expedition was led by Guinn Harris Heap. The other, the official expedition, was led by Captain John W. Gunnison. It was the second of these that Fremont had hoped to lead. Always strong-willed and independent, Fremont believed that the other two would prove valueless, for they were being undertaken in the summer, a season when a railroad would have little difficulty crossing the San Juan Mountains, a formidable range in any season but one that could present impossible problems in winter. Without a winter survey, Fremont reasoned, the other two expeditions would prove nothing.

When Carvalho joined the Fremont party, his family had questioned the wisdom of putting his life in the hands of a man like Fremont—born out of wedlock, a "mountaineer," an "adventurer," and a "man of no education." But Carvalho saw Fremont differently, as a man of "high literary attainments," "great mental capacity," and "solid scientific knowledgements"—not only a "man of education" but a "man of genius and a gentleman"—"reserved almost to taciturnity yet perfectly amiable withal."[7]

Fremont enthusiastically began making preparations for his expedition, buying surveying instruments and field equipment, engaging the men to fill key posts on the expedition. With Carvalho on board, the question of who was going to operate the complicated daguerreotype equipment was seemingly answered. At all costs, Fremont wanted to be the first explorer to have a complete photographic record of an expedition. It had been his search for a competent daguerreotypist that led him to Carvalho.[8]

Within a few weeks after being engaged by Fremont, Carvalho set out for St. Louis, carrying his painting supplies and his unwieldy daguerreotype equipment. Here he rendezvoused with Fremont and a few key members of the exploring party. There was F. W. von Egglofstein, the chief topographer and, like Carvalho, a Jew;[9] Oliver Fuller, his assistant; and a man named Bomar, also a photographer.[10] Bomar's presence no doubt came as a shock to Carvalho. But Fremont did not want to take any chances with his photographic record, and Bomar's method, a wax process, was entirely different from Carvalho's. Fremont explained that he would choose between the two men before the expedition got underway. Together the five men boarded the steamer, F.X. Audrey, bound for Kansas.[11]

By September 15, the entire Fremont party had arrived at Westport (Kansas City), ready to head westward. While camped here, Fremont got the news that the Heap-Beale expedition was already in Colorado and had crossed Cochetopa Pass. Fremont quickly dismissed the news as unimportant. What had to be proved was that Cochetopa Pass, at the Continental Divide, could be crossed in the dead of winter.[12]

There was still the matter to be decided of who would be the official photographer—Bomar with his wax process or Carvalho, using the daguerreotype method? Fremont held a contest between the two men, with speed being the deciding factor. Bomar's wax process required more time and would have caused delays. Carvalho was declared the winner, and became the expedition's official photographer.[13]

By September 20, the full complement of men had arrived at Westport. The Fremont party consisted of ten Delaware Indians, two Mexicans, several muleskinners, plus the officers—von Egglofstein, Oliver Fuller, Max Strobel, W. H. Palmer and Carvalho. The Delawares, who all spoke English, had such names as Washington, Welluchas, Solomon and Moses. All were under the command of a Delaware chief, one Captain Wolff, who referred to himself as the "Big Indian." Each man in the party was issued a rifle and a Colt revolver.[14]

The Delawares loved Fremont, their "Great Captain," because he was a firm but fair leader who would not ask a man to take a chance that he himself would not take. The Indians, to a man, would have laid down their lives for him.

There was great concern and disappointment, therefore, when Fremont became ill shortly after the expedition left Westport and had to return to St. Louis for medical treatment. Before leaving, he turned over the command to W. H. Palmer, and left instructions for the expedition to proceed to the Grand Saline Fork of the Kansas River, in Kansas Territory, close to where Sigmund Shlesinger would distinguish himself, fifteen years later, at the Battle of Beecher Island.

It was not until late October that Fremont would arrive at the rendezvous point, fully recovered, to resume his leadership role. Finally ready to proceed, the expedition, whose members were greatly relieved to have Fremont back in command, headed out toward Bent's Fort and the snow-covered peaks of the Rocky Mountains.[15]

The delay caused by Fremont's illness turned out not to be a serious setback. Nothing was lost. A fearsome winter still lay ahead, no matter what. It would take six months for the expedition to reach San Francisco, its destination. To get there, the Fremont party would journey through Kansas, and cut across the lower part of Colorado to Bent's Fort. From there it would cross the Rockies at Cochetopa Pass and march south to the San Juan Mountains in southwest Colorado. Then, after crossing into Utah, it would traverse the treacherous canyonlands into the Mormon settlement at Parowan. The route out of Utah would take the party due west across Nevada to the southern edge of the Sierra Nevada Mountains, and then north to San Francisco.

During the journey, Carvalho would have some memorable experiences among the Indians, some pleasant, some harrowing. Certainly, very few Jews had ever marched over the perilous route that Carvalho had traversed, and none, to be sure, had carried cameras.

Shortly after Fremont returned to his men in Kansas Territory, the winter of 1853 now beginning to close in, Carvalho would have his first encounter with unfriendly Indians. One especially cold night, Fremont personally inspected the guard, choosing a time when he would be least expected. Finding the guard post unmanned, Fremont asked the officer on duty if he had, for any reason, relieved the guard. The officer hadn't, but explained that the cold weather probably accounted for the guard's absence at the exact time Fremont arrived. Surely, it was a coincidence. It seemed probable that the guard had gone for a moment to warm his hands at the campfire. Fremont was irate. He fiercely chastised the officer on duty and sentenced the guard to walk the following day instead of riding his mule.[16]

Despite his great admiration for Fremont, Carvalho thought the punishment disproportionately severe. After all, the poor guard had only gone to the campfire to warm his hands. Carvalho found out later, however, that the guard's minor infraction had had serious consequences. A party of Cheyenne had evidently been watching the Fremont camp in the night and had stolen five mules in the brief time the guard had left his post. The Delawares later tracked down the Cheyenne and recovered the stolen mules. From then on, Carvalho never questioned an order by Fremont. The incident had reassured Carvalho. Because of Fremont's watchfulness and experience, the artist could trek less fearfully through country in which hostile Comanche and Pawnee were ever present predators.[17]

While journeying through Kansas, Carvalho had the chance to ingratiate himself with Captain Wolff, the Delaware chief. The chief had fallen ill, and noticing some unusual activity taking place, Carvalho was told by one of the Delawares that a "great medicine man" was performing the Indian ceremony of "incantation" in an effort to cure the chief. The rite was performed by making an almost air-tight hut of tree branches with just enough room for one man to sit upright inside. The chief, totally naked, sat in the hut, smoking a pipe filled with a mixture of tobacco and "kinnickinick" (dried sumach leaves), puffing frenziedly so that huge drafts of smoke filled his lungs and beclouded the enclosure. The medicine man, standing outside the enclosure, recited powerful words while the smoke filled the enclosure so completely that the poor chief, on the verge of asphyxiation, had to be conveyed to his own tent, gasping for air.[18]

Concerned about Captain Wolff, Carvalho entered his tent and found him in a state of great agitation, a condition that he was certain had been brought about by the bizarre treatment at the hands of the medicine man. The chief complained of headache and backpain, and was certain that he was going to die. Carvalho asked that he be given a chance to make the chief well, and the Indian, not having a reasonable alternative, gladly consented. Now it so happened that Carvalho carried with him an extraordinary assortment of supplies—medicines, Havana cigars, cognac. He opened his wooden supply box and quickly administered ten grains of calomel to the chief. Four hours later, he returned and gave the Indian a half ounce of epsom salts. The chief began to recover almost immediately. Carvalho had correctly diagnosed the ailment as indigestion. As soon as he saw the chief responding, he reached once again into his supply box and gave him some arrowroot. "If I had not treated him, "he wrote in his diary, "he probably would have died. Another incantation would certainly have killed him."[19] Carvalho, the "Jewish mother," had triumphed over the medicine man.

Carvalho, thanks to the Delawares, gradually was able to adapt to camp life. For one thing, he learned how to build a fire with "buffalo chips"—dried dung that, when ignited, burns hot and slow and retains heat longer than wood. "A peculiar smell exhales from it while burning," Carvalho wrote, "[and it is] not at all unpleasant."[20] The Delawares also taught Carvalho the secret of cooking buffalo meat; of preparing "kinnikinick"—a good substitute smoke—and of how to excel in playing various Indian games.[21]

The Delawares were great hunters, and during the time they were waiting for Fremont's return from Westport, had taught Carvalho, by now an expert rifle shot, how to hunt buffalo. Early one morning, Carvalho had joined a party of Delawares on a buffalo hunt. After waiting patiently for over three hours in the cold fall morning, Carvalho and the Indians came upon a large herd of the animals, steers, cows and calves alike, and the entire party galloped after them. Carvalho, who preferred cow meat to steer meat because the flesh was more tender, chased after what he believed to be a cow. After a two mile chase, he fired his rifle, wounding the animal in the leg. Closing in for the kill, he took out his Colt revolver and fired again, only to discover that he had killed an old bull instead. After Carvalho told the story around the campfire that evening, Captain Wolff laughed, and informed Carvalho that he had not killed a buffalo at all, neither bull nor cow. To the Indians, when something isn't done according to Indian ritual, then it isn't done at all. The Delaware chief explained: "When Captain Wolff kill buffalo, he cut out tongue. Indian shoot buffalo, bring home tongue. Carvalho no bring buffalo tongue, he no kill buffalo."[22]

As the expedition moved deeper into Kansas Territory, the weather turned cold and disagreeable. For Carvalho to make daguerreotypes in the open air, with temperatures dipping down to thirty-below zero, was a far more complicated task than making them in the warm climate of South Carolina or the Barbados, where Carvalho had gained his experience and skill. Despite the fact that the daguerreotype was faster than Bomar's wax process, the heavy weight of the daguerreotype equipment and the slow setting up process caused delays in the expedition while Carvalho photographed.

As difficult as the artist's photographic duties were, they did not excuse him from other duties. Carvalho explained in his diary:

> The duties of camp life are becoming more onerous as the weather gets colder. It's expected that each man in camp will bring in a certain quantity of firewood! My turn came today, and I'm afraid I shall make a poor hand in using the axe; first, I have not the physical strength, and secondly, I do not know how...I certainly, being a Republican, do not expect to warm myself at the expense of another; therefore, arduous as it is, I must, to carry out the principle of equality, do as the rest do, although it is not a very congenial occupation.[23]

The Fremont expedition followed the Arkansas River, and while on this course, in west central Kansas, it arrived at a

Cheyenne village, populated, Carvalho estimated, by approximately a thousand men, women and children. Carvalho made daguerreotype pictures of the teepees, and despite having a hard time getting the Indians to sit still, managed to get photographs of an Indian princess, an old woman and several chiefs. He later showed them the daguerreotypes, and from then on, he indicated in his diary, "I was a supernatural being."[24]

The Indians were shortly to become convinced beyond doubt that Carvalho was no mere mortal. The Indian princess was a beauty, and for the picture-taking session had bedecked herself in her finest clothing. She had put on colorful robes, appliqued with elks teeth, porcupine quills and beads. On her arms were bracelets of brass, obtained from traders and trappers who had passed through the village. Silver jewelry was a rarity, and few Indians, even the daughter of a chief, could claim such a prize. Noting her brass bracelets, Carvalho asked the princess if he might borrow one. Reluctantly she handed it over. Carvalho carefully wiped the bracelet clean, then, opening his wooden supply box, took out his quicksilver and applied a small amount to the bracelet. The bracelet was instantly transformed from brass into what looked like glistening silver. Incredulous and elated, the princess danced for joy as she admired the glittering bracelet on her arm. Now other Indian women excitedly gathered around Carvalho, holding their brass bracelets out to the artist; and soon Carvalho became the great magician, the man who could miraculously change brass to silver, and the astonished Indians implored Carvalho to stay on and live with them forever.[25]

While with the Cheyennes, Carvalho witnessed an impressive spectacle: the return of the Cheyenne warriors from a successful battle with the Pawnees, their deadliest enemies. As part of the celebration, the Cheyenne performed a scalp dance, in which more than a dozen Pawnee scalps, dangling from poles, were the focal point of the victory rite. The men and women of the village wore wolf, bear and buffalo robes, and, as head ornaments, deer antlers and buffalo horns. They danced, howled and chanted around a huge fire, their faces streaked with red and black paint.

Carvalho watched the ghoulish rite impassively, and, as a man of cultivated sensibility, noted only that the Indians simply had no instinct for music because they all sang in a monotone.[26]

About seventy miles east of the Rockies, close to where Lamar, Colorado is now located, was the site of the then new Bent's Fort, an important Santa Fe trail outpost for traders, Indians and trappers. The original fort, farther to the west, had been destroyed by its owner, William Bent, after a dispute with the government. The expedition stayed for a short time at the new fort while Fremont stocked up with supplies—fresh mules for each man, dried buffalo meat, overshoes, sugar, coffee and buffalo robes. The cold was already bitter and would get worse, and Fremont and his men would need all the food and cold weather gear William Bent could supply them with.[27]

Their supplies in hand, the expedition now proceeded across the Huerfano River toward the base of the Rockies, the glistening white summit of Pikes Peak off in the distant northwest. While here, Carvalho and Fremont left the party to search for impressive scenes for photography. Among those photographed were Huerfano Butte, and off in the distance San Luis Valley and the San Juan Mountains. Some of the views were so spectacular that they could be improved upon only by scaling snow covered peaks. Fremont wanted all of the views but didn't want to ascend farther, but, as Carvalho reports in his diary, he himself, stunned by the breathtaking view of the Rockies, was insistent upon climbing higher.

> Standing as it were in the vestibule of God's holy temple, I
> forgot I was of this mundane sphere; the divine part of man
> elevated itself undisturbed by the influences of the world. I
> looked from nature up to nature's God, more chastened
> and purified than I ever felt before.[28]

The expedition inched its way up the Sangre Cristo Mountains, and then into the San Luis Valley, finally reaching Cochetopa Pass on December 14, 1853. Fremont, Egloffstein, Fuller and Strobel took the necessary sightings and made sketches for their maps. Carvalho took numerous daguerreotypes.[29] Having reached the Continental Divide, the expedition would now have to make its descent. Icy winds and heavy snow would make the long descent to Colorado's western slope very treacherous. To add to its problems, the expedition's supply of food was beginning to run out. On New Year's day, 1854, Carvalho, who hadn't as yet exhausted his bag of tricks, pulled out a surprise. He had brought with him two boxes of preserved eggs and milk in hermetically sealed tin cans. No one knew he had these rare items. In honor of New Year's day, he combined sugar, milk and eggs with six gallons of boiling water, and "made as fine a *blanc mange* as ever was *manged* on Mount Blanc...six gallons of nourishing food, sweetened and flavored,"[30] enough to serve each man on the expedition.

The Fremont party was again underway. It moved slowly across the western slope of Colorado and crossed the Grand River at the Colorado-Utah frontier. The men were now a ragged group. Fremont, their imperturbable leader, did his best to encourage his men, but they were tired and miserably cold, and were becoming increasingly concerned with their own survival. In a few days they would reach the red canyonlands of eastern Utah and cross the Green River, but by then they would have shot all twenty-seven of their horses for food and would journey the rest of the way on foot, in bitter cold, their boots wearing thin.

With the worst still to come, Carvalho, the snow above his knees, made his way up the mountain slope to round up the stray horses. He reached under his buffalo robes and pulled out a miniature of his wife and children, gazing at the picture sadly, bitterly regretting his decision to accompany Fremont on the expedition. It was then that he thought of his mother and her words. "Dear Soul, how her heart would have ached for him..."[31]

Cold, tired and hungry, Carvalho made his way back to camp. He warmed his hands before the fire and lay down under his buffalo robes, thinking of "warm rooms, "feather beds" and the "silken canopy" of his wedding chamber.[32]

The scientific duties of Egloffstein, Fuller and Carvalho

required them to bring up the rear of the party. By now, the expedition was approaching the Green River. Fuller, whose horse had given out and had been shot for food, had been on foot longer than any man in the party and could not continue. His boots were so worn out that the flesh of his feet was exposed. Carvalho and Egloffstein, themselves on foot and burdened with their equipment, had no choice but to leave Fuller behind while they sought help. Fremont, on hearing of Fuller's plight, sent two Delawares to rescue him, but by the time Fuller was returned to camp, it was too late. His legs were frozen black, and only his eventual death saved him from amputation. Fuller had been the strongest man in camp when the expedition left Westport, and appeared to be much better equipped to bear the hardships of the journey than any other man. Carvalho noted the irony: he himself, the weakest of them all, was alive to chronicle Fuller's sufferings.[33]

On February 8, 1854, the expedition finally reached Parowan, Utah, a small Mormon settlement in the Little Salt Lake Valley. Salt Lake City was three-hundred miles to the north, San Bernardino, California, five-hundred miles southwest. Parowan's population when Fremont's ragged party staggered into the village was one-hundred Mormon families. The expedition had suffered through heavy snow drifts, freezing cold and intense hunger. They were tired and emaciated. Carvalho was ill, suffering from diarrhea and displaying symptoms of scurvy. His clothes were in tatters, his hair long and matted, and he had become skeleton-thin. The people of Parowan mistook him for an Indian. The most difficult part of the journey was over, but neither Carvalho nor Egloffstein were in any condition to continue with Fremont, and had to leave the expedition.[34]

Fremont and his men stayed on in Parowan for two weeks. During that time, the men were fed and clothed by the Mormons, and Carvalho was partially restored to health. It was while still at Parowan that Fremont learned that the Gunnison expedition had failed, and that John Gunnison himself had been killed by the Indians.[35]

The day Fremont departed from Parowan, Carvalho and

Egloffstein, both still in fragile health, set out for Salt Lake City, riding in a wagon with a group of Mormons on their way to "Conference."

Carvalho remained in Salt Lake City for ten weeks where he gradually regained his health. He got on splendidly with the Mormons, and though he deplored the practice of polygamy, he believed that the Mormons had many admirable qualities. The city of Salt Lake itself told the story. It had a population of fifteen-thousand, and Carvalho marveled that, during his stay, he never heard any obscene language, never saw anybody drunk, saw no brothels, no grog shops, and no gambling halls.[36]

While in Salt Lake, Egloffstein, the topographical engineer, accepted employment with Lieutenant Beckwith of the Gunnison expedition, to replace an engineer slain by the Indians.[37]

The territory of Utah, which included Nevada and western Colorado, was organized in 1850, and Brigham Young was appointed governor. He had great success as a peacemaker for the various warring tribes, and in Carvalho's view made good headway as well in soothing the hostile feelings of Indians toward the white immigrants. His efforts to convert the Indians to Mormonism were not successful, however. All the kindnesses he would extend to Carvalho, however, were not undertaken with conversion in mind. The Mormons believe Jews are God's chosen people, and identify their members as descendants of Abraham, Isaac and Jacob, so conversion is unnecessary.[38]

Young, who had nineteen wives and innumerable children, took Carvalho under his wing, and invited the artist to live in his home.[39] During his stay, Carvalho was invited by Young to attend a grand ball. Despite that fact that his own clothing was in tatters and inappropriate for so elegant an occasion, Carvalho some-how managed to show up as fashionably attired as any man in attendance. The resourceful artist had somehow obtained striped "cassimere" trousers, a black frock coat and white vest.[40]

The day of the ball, Carvalho dined at the home of Ezra Taft Benson, where Benson's wives were busily preparing food—roasting wild geese, baking, and "garnishing fat hams" for the ball.[41]

Young graciously gave Carvalho a general introduction at the ball, and invited the artist to dance with one of his wives. "A larger collection of fairer and more beautiful women I never saw in one room," Carvalho wrote. But, he added, "the utmost order and strictest decorum prevailed." Polkas and waltzes and other one on one dancing were not permitted. Quadrilles, cotillions and country dancing were allowed, however.[42]

Carvalho painted several portraits while in Salt Lake City—two of Brigham Young, and several of officials of the Mormon church.[43]

On May 6, 1854, Carvalho left Salt Lake, bound for San Bernardino and Los Angeles. Young wanted Carvalho to have a safe escort, so the artist left with a party of twenty-three Mormon missionaries. Their route would take them on a southwest course through various Mormon settlements in Utah.[44] Along the way there would be a brief rendezvous with Young in Provost City (Provo). The governor had promised to wait for Carvalho there before having a parley with Walkara, the great Ute Indian chief. Relations had been strained between the Mormons and the Indians, resulting in bloody clashes, and deaths on both sides.[45] Captain John Gunnison was killed in revenge for the wanton slaying of an Indian by white immigrants on their way to California. The Indians in the area, the Utahs, the Paiutes and the Pavants were committed to revenge against all white men, including the Mormons. But Major Biddell, the Indian agent, had been able to persuade the Indians to suspend their war on the white man until Brigham Young, the great white leader, could meet Walkara, the great Ute chief.[46]

Carvalho writes of eventually catching up with Young at a Mormon settlement nineteen miles south of Provost City, and of being greeted warmly by the Mormon leader. In Young's party were Ezra Taft Benson, along with several apostles and advisers, "fifty men on mounts and one hundred wagons and teams filled with gentlemen with their wives and families."[47] Completing the party was the Jew, Solomon Carvalho. The tribal chiefs, together with the Young contingent, were to meet at Walkara's camp, outside of the village of Nephi.[48]

Young brought with him an assortment of valuable gifts for the Indians—sixteen head of cattle, blankets, clothing, trinkets, even arms and ammunition. Carvalho questioned Young about the wisdom of furnishing firearms to the Indians, but Young replied that the purpose was to give the Indians the means of shooting their own game. And besides, Young added, the Indians were already well-armed and quite expert in the use of rifles.[49]

Young sent word of his arrival to Walkara, apparently with the implied request that Walkara travel to the Young encampment outside of Provost City. Walkara would have none of that. The chief's attitude was that he had been the injured party in all the strife, and was therefore indifferent to the outcome of the parley. He promptly sent word back that if the governor wanted to see him, the governor would have to come to Walkara.[50]

When the Young party finally arrived, they were greeted by such famous chiefs as Ammon, Squash-Head, Grosepine, Petetnit and Kanosh, and were then invited into Walkara's tent, Carvalho in attendance.[51]

Walkara, wrapped in a blanket and sitting on his buffalo robes, waved to Young and beckoned him to sit at his side. After introductions were made, the chiefs immediately began to vent their rage, describing in detail their grievances against the Mormons and other white men, recounting tales of Indian women having been murdered and of sons killed in battle. Young made his plea for peace. Walkara remained silent, but finally announced that he would consult with the Great Spirit and render a decision on the following day.[52]

When the peace parley resumed the next day, Walkara was visibly tired. He had spent the night carefully examining all issues. Should the Indians declare war on the Mormons and all other white men, or should there be peace? He said to Young that he had been wrongly accused of killing Captain Gunnison, an accusation which made him "sore at heart." But, the Great Spirit had counseled: "Make peace. When Mormon first come to live on Walkara's land, Walkara give him welcome. He give Walkara plenty bread and clothes...Walkara no want to fight

Mormon. Mormon chief very good man."[53]

With Walkara's decision delivered, the peace pipe was passed around, and the council concluded. Carvalho in the meantime had been sketching the various chiefs,[54] and later persuaded Walkara to sit for a portrait, the same portrait that today hangs at the Gilcrease Museum in Tulsa, Oklahoma.

When they left Walkara's camp, Carvalho and the Young party set out for Fillmore City, thirty-five miles to the south. There, Carvalho, accompanied by two interpreters, headed straight for the Pavant Indian camp to see Kanosh, their chief, because Carvalho wanted to paint the chief's portrait. Carvalho writes of their meeting:

> I found him well-armed with a rifle and pistols and mounted on a noble horse. He has a Roman nose with fine intelligent cast of countenance, and his thick black hair is brushed off his forehead, contrary to the usual custom of the table. He immediately consented to my request that he would sit for his portrait, and on the spot, after an hour's labor, I produced a strong likeness of him which he was very curious to see. I opened my portfolio and displayed portraits of a number of chiefs, among which he selected Walkara. He took hold of it and wanted to retain it. It was, he said, "weino"—a contraction of the Spanish "bueno"— very good.[55]

The Pavant chief then told Carvalho the details surrounding the massacre of Captain Gunnison. It was actually his own tribe, the Pavants, who had done it, although Kanosh himself was not involved. Gunnison's death, however, was justified, the chief pointed out, because it was an act of revenge for the death of an old Pavant chief by one of Gunnison's [sic] party.[56]

Carvalho continued his journey south, finally reaching Parowan, the small Mormon settlement where he first arrived cold and emaciated after his journey over the mountains with Fremont. The same people who had cared for him during his illness a few months earlier were on hand to greet him. They were, of course, a bit startled to see a much more robust and healthy Carvalho, and at first had not recognized him.[57]

The day after he arrived, Carvalho, while taking a stroll though the village, his sketchbook in hand, noticed a distraught man, pacing back and forth in front of a small shack. Carvalho approached the man and, because he looked so troubled, asked what was wrong. The man said his only daughter, six years old, had died suddenly during the night. He asked Carvalho to step inside the shack.

Carvalho spotted the dead child's body lying on a straw mattress, and was struck by her beauty. "She was one of the most angelic children I ever saw," he wrote, "...beautiful curls clustered around a brow of snowy whiteness. It was easy to perceive that it was a child lately from England from its peculiar conformation." The child's mother was reclining on a bed, sobbing in her pillow.

Carvalho immediately began sketching the child; his hand going to his pad as if drawn by some outside force, so overcome was the artist by the child's beauty. In a short time he had produced an excellent likeness of the child. The mother, who had not seen Carvalho come into the room, now took notice of him. Carvalho explained that he was part of the Brigham Young party, and had arrived the previous evening. With that he handed the mother the sketch of her daughter. "It is impossible to describe the delight and joy she expressed at its possession," Carvalho wrote. "She said I was an angel sent from heaven to comfort her. She had no likeness of her child."

The next day, while Carvalho was preparing for his journey to San Bernardino, he found a basket filled with eggs, butter and several loaves of bread in his wagon. A note was in the basket. It read: "From a grateful heart."[58]

Carvalho said goodbye to Brigham Young in Parowan, and began his journey to San Bernardino with a party of Mormon missionaries. He eventually reached Los Angeles where during his short visit he was instrumental in forming the Los Angeles Hebrew Benevolent Society. At its first meeting the society passed a resolution of thanks in Carvalho's honor:

Los Angeles, California—At a meeting of the Israelites of
the city of Los Angeles, held on this 2nd of July, 1854, for
the purpose of forming a charitable society by the name of
"Hebrew Benevolent Society" and for the purpose of
obtaining a piece of land for a Jewish graveyard, the
following officers were elected: S.K. Labatt, President;
Charles Shachro, Vice President; Hyam Goldberg and
S. Lazard, Trustees; and Jacob Elias, Secretary.

It was resolved unanimously that the thanks of this meeting
be tendered to Mr. S.N. Carvalho for his valuable services
in organizing the Society, and that he be elected an honor-
ary member; also, that these proceedings be published in
The Occident.[59]

After leaving Parowan on Febru-
ary 21, 1854, Colonel Fremont and his party, Carvalho and
Egloffstein, its two Jewish members absent, followed the wagon
route to Cedar City, Utah, then moved toward the Escalante
Desert, entering Nevada near the village of Pioche. The expedi-
tion reached the Sierra Nevada range at what is now Bishop,
California, eventually arriving at the San Joachin Valley and then
San Francisco.[60]

Fremont hailed his expedition a success. His trailblazing
journey would serve well as a year 'round railroad route. A major
advantage of the route was that along the way there were big
stands of timber in addition to rich deposits of coal and iron.[61]
The human cost of the expedition, however, had been a heavy
one. Provisions were scanty. The men went hungry for days at a
time, pack animals went lame and were eventually eaten. The
scientist, Fuller, had died on the trail.[62]

Solomon Nunes Carvalho had
come from an old Sephardic Jewish family whose origins were
Spanish and Portugese. The family had lived in England for
several generations. Carvalho's father, David Nunes Carvalho,
also an artist as well as a man of literary taste, was born in London
in 1784. In 1814, he married Sarah D'Azevedo of Charleston,

and a year later, on April 27, 1815, the first child, Solomon, was born. David and Sarah had four more children during the next twenty years—Emmanuel, Isaac, Sarah and Julia. Isaac, the last born, did not survive infancy.[63]

Carvalho was reared in Charleston, at that time a prosperous port and center of culture and trade. He was educated at Charleston College and at local religious schools.[64] His education was well grounded in the classics, and he knew Latin and Greek as well as Hebrew.[65] David and Sarah placed great value on secular and Jewish culture, and Carvalho, throughout his life, pursued these things with great vigor. Between 1828 and 1860, Carvalho moved around a great deal, residing for various periods in Philadelphia, Baltimore, Charleston, Barbados, Los Angeles and New York. After his father's death in 1860, he moved his family to New York permanently. Carvalho was then forty-five. In New York he would achieve the financial success that had eluded him as an artist by operating a steam and hot water heating business, using products that he had invented.[66]

David and Sarah Carvalho had moved from Charleston to Baltimore in 1828 when Solomon was thirteen. Seven years later, the family moved once again, this time to Philadelphia. Solomon, now approaching twenty, was sent to Barbados to live with and work for an uncle in the importing business. In 1838, while still living in Barbados, he sold his first painting, an interior of the Charleston synagogue which he had painted from memory.[67] It would be the first of well over sixty of his works—portraits, landscapes, photographs and sketches—that exist today in various public and private collections. His portrait of Abraham Lincoln, commissioned by the president and among his best known, is at Brandeis University. A portrait of Judah Touro hangs at the Touro Infirmary in New Orleans; and his celebrated portrait of Walkara, the chief's hair brushed down on his forehead, has a startling impact on visitors to the Gilcrease Museum.[68]

Other portraits include those of Brigham Young; Judah P. Benjamin, the Confederate patriot; Dr. David Camden DeLeon, first surgeon general of the Confederate army; Don Pio Pico,

Spanish governor of California; Paul Morphy, the American chess grandmaster, friend and occasional chess opponent of Carvalho; and Isaac Leeser, the sephardic rabbi, editor of *The Occident* and spirtual force behind the founding of Dropsie College.

Several of Carvalho's paintings were rendered from sketches on his expedition with Fremont. These include "View in the Cochetope Pass, Rocky Mountains, Discovered by Colonel Fremont;" "Entrance to the Valley of St. Clare, Between Utah and California;" and "Sunset on the Los Angeles River." Most of Carvalho's photography and sketches of the expedition were lost and have never been located, although it is said that some plates are still in unopened crates at the National Archives, mixed with those of Matthew Brady, the Civil War photographer.[69]

Carvalho's painting, "Child With Rabbits," later was used as an embellishment on widely circulated bank notes in the United States and Canada in the 1850's and 1860's.[70]

Carvalho not only invented a heating process but also a process to protect daguerreotype plates. Isaac Leeser wrote in *The Occident:*

> Mr. S.N. Carvalho has invented a method of varnishing daguerreotypes which will protect them against abrasion and dispense with the necessity of covering them with glass. It is not often that persons of our persuasion turn their attention to inventions and mechanical contrivances; wherefore we seize the first leisure we have to record them in our magazine.[71]

Carvalho, the writer, was a contributor to *The Occident.* In addition, he wrote long theological treatises, including one on "Mosaic Cosmogony," referring to the picture of the universe portrayed in the first five books of the Bible. In addition to his book, *Incidents of Travel,* he was the author of a history of the Isle of Martinique, which appeared in *Harper's Monthly.*

Owing to his association with Fremont, Carvalho's *Incidents of Travel* became an instant success when it first appeared in 1856. Offered by the publisher a choice of a flat payment of three-hundred dollars or royalties of five-cents per copy, Carvalho, in need of money, accepted the flat payment. It proved to be an unwise decision because of the book's wide acceptance.

In 1845, nine years before he left for the West, Carvalho had married Sarah Marion Solis, fourth daughter of Jacob Fonseca D'Silva Solis whose ancestry dated back to twelfth century Spain. Their wedding notice in *The Occident* read:

> On Wednesday the 15th of October, at the residence of
> Mr. S. Solis, Mr. Solomon N. Carvalho of Bridgetown,
> Barbados, and son of Mr. D. N. Carvalho of Philadelphia,
> to Miss Sarah M. Solis of the city, daughter of the late
> Jacob S. Solis.[72]

Sarah's father was dead, so Solomon had to turn to her brother to seek her hand in marriage. Carvalho's elegant writing style was never more evident than in his letter to Solomon Solis:

> For your esteemed sister, Sarah, I have conceived other
> than mere commonplace feelings. Her amiability, sweetness
> of temper, together with a congeniality of disposition and I
> dare hope a reciprocity of sentiment, have awakened in my
> bosom feelings of a deep and ardent affection and as her
> guardian and Elder Brother, I deem it a duty I owe you, to
> acquaint you with my pretensions, and to obtain your
> sanction that I may make her Honorable proposals of
> Marriage, the consummation of which would render me
> most happy.[73]

After his marriage, Carvalho began seriously to devote himself to art and photography. He gained some acclaim during the next several years but not much wealth. His reputation as an artist and daguerreotypist reached Fremont, and eight years after his marriage, he would say goodbye to Sarah and to their three young children, David, Jacob and Charity,[74] and at the age of thirty-eight, begin his memorable journey over the Rockies.

In 1855, the newly formed Republican party asked Fremont, his successful fifth expedition behind him, to be a candidate for president. He was thought to be the ideal choice. The Republicans had a strong anti-slavery stance, just as Fremont had, and, moreover, because of his successful expedition, Fremont was an idealized and romantic hero to most Americans.[75] Fremont was officially nominated on June 19, 1856 at the Republican convention in Philadelphia. His running mate, Senator William L. Dayton of New Jersey, edged out Abraham Lincoln for second place on the ticket. The other presidential candidates were James Buchanan for the Democrats and Millard Fillmore for the Whigs.

Fremont was a quiet and introspective man, more at home around a campfire than on the campaign trail. He was promoted excessively and glorified in prose and verse by Horace Greeley and John Greenleaf Whittier. Fremont, who wanted to discuss substantive issues, was unable to deal in the flip generalities and sloganeering the voters wanted to hear.

Meanwhile, Carvalho was capitalizing on Fremont's campaign. In New York at the time his book, *Incidents of Travel*, was published, Carvalho campaigned vigorously for Fremont. He addressed Fremont supporters in large street gatherings and basked in Fremont's glory. "Three cheers for Carvalho, the Fremont expedition artist," the crowds would yell. "Hip, Hip, Hooray!"[76] Flushed by the success of his book, Carvalho began besporting himself around New York, dining in elegant restaurants and smoking "a dozen four-cent cigars daily," enjoying his new-found fame. He anticipated being appointed Collector of the Port of Baltimore when Fremont became president.[77]

But it was not to be. Fremont's opponents slammed him unmercifully—for his illegitimate birth, for his Catholic upbringing (even though he was an Episcopalian), and for his failed fourth expedition. He lost to Buchanan who carried nineteen states. Fremont carried eleven, Fillmore eight. It was a respectable showing.[78]

From the time of his defeat until the outbreak of the Civil War, Fremont and his wife, Jessie, lived a quiet and fashionable life in San Francisco. When the war broke out, he was commissioned a major general in the Union army, commanding the Department of the West, headquartered in St. Louis.[79] Fremont, first and always a dreamer and trailblazer, had the misfortune of confronting Stonewall Jackson in battle, and even though Fremont's military encounter with Jackson was an impossibly difficult one, his defeat resulted in disgrace. Lincoln, now president, placed Fremont's troops under the command of General John Pope.[80]

Because of Fremont's popularity, his dismissal by Lincoln was not politically prudent, and accordingly the president gave Fremont another post, this in March, 1862, as commander of the Mountain Department. But this assignment was also ill-fated, and again Fremont lost his appointment.[81]

After the war, because of a series of poor business ventures, Fremont's financial position became desperate. He lived off the writings of his wife, Jessie, and a small salary as territorial governor of Arizona. After he died penniless in 1890, John Charles Fremont nevertheless continued to be a symbol of freedom and adventure to the American people; and until the very last, Fremont, the trailblazer of the West, kept on dreaming of further expeditions.

Carvalho, who made his home in New York after 1861, was in New Orleans at the outbreak of the Civil War. The reason for his trip was to introduce his new steam-heating process to the South, and, while there, to try to sell prayer books for Isaac Leeser and to solicit subscriptions for Leeser's periodical, *The Occident.* It was during this trip that he painted the portrait of Judah Touro.

His process for heating with hot water and steam eventually became quite successful. It was promoted as "An Entirely New Steam Super-Heating System By Hot Water Circulating Under Pressure" The invention won Carvalho the Medal of Excellence by the American Institute of New York.[82] He began calling himself "Professor," and became president of The Carvalho Heating Company in New York in 1867. He continued to paint until 1870 when failing eyesight ended his career as an artist.

In 1897, at the age of eighty-two, Solomon Nunes Carvalho, official artist and photographer for Fremont's fifth expedition, died peacefully in New York. His paintings and photographs, which are valued treasures today in libraries, museums and private collections, only tell part of the story of this Jewish Leonardo. But to those who cherish the exploits of the trailblazing heroes of the West, Carvalho, the man who painted Indians, was also one of the first Jews to cross the Rockies, a Jewish medicine man extraordinary, a man who hunted buffalo with the Indians, who magically transformed brass bracelets to silver, and who sat with Brigham Young and Chief Walkara at the truce powwow between the Mormons and the Utes.

He and his wife, Sarah, who died three years before him, are buried in Shearith Israel Synagogue cemetery in New York—a long, long way from Cochetopa Pass.

Notes

Chapter 1 Notes

1   Buffalo Bill's Wild West Show appeared in Cleveland in 1897 and again in 1901. The "programme" for the 1897 show, which was secured from the Cleveland Historical Society, was printed specifically for the troupe's New York appearance in the same year. Thus, the line-up of acts was the same for both cities.

2   Three of the twenty-two acts printed on the "programme" were concerned with depicting Indian attacks on white settlers.

3   Sigmund and Fannie Shlesinger had three children — Lillian (Mrs. Max) Frankenberger of Charleston, West Virginia; Louis Shlesinger of Cleveland, and Albert Shlesinger of Fremont, Ohio. Albert, the youngest, was not born at the time Buffalo Bill appeared in Cleveland.

4   Letter from Lillian Frankenberger to Dr. Jacob Rader Marcus, February 1, 1967. American Jewish Archives.

5   Ibid.

6   The Battle of Beecher Island had additional significance. It was only one of a few times in which western Indians had departed from their customary tactics of sudden incursion and rapid flight by engaging, all throttles open, in a pitched battle against an organized body of white soldiers. One exception was the charge at Fort Supply, Oklahoma; another at the Cimarron-crossing on the Arkansas River, and still another at the Battle on the Little Big Horn.

7   Merrill J. Mattes, "The Beecher Island Battlefield Diary of Sigmund Shlesinger," *The Colorado Magazine,* July 1952. American Jewish Archives, Cincinnati.

8   General George A. Forsyth, "A Frontier Fight," *Harper's Magazine,* 1900. Reprinted in *The Beecher Island Annual*:5, ed. Robert Lynam (Wray, Colorado: The Beecher Island Battle Memorial Association, September, 1917).

9   Ibid.

10   General James B. Fry, *Army and Navy Magazine,* April 26, 1893, quoted by Burt A. Siegel, "The Little Jew Was There," *American Jewish Archives*:20, no.1, April 1968.

11   Frederick Beecher had served with gallantry in the Civil War. He was wounded in the knee at Gettysburg, a wound that left him permanently lame. He was well-liked and highly regarded as an officer by both Sheridan and Forsyth. His superiors, however, were aware that Beecher, in recent times, had developed a fondness for liquor, and

Forsyth was therefore apprehensive about the lieutenant. He feared that alcohol might somehow distort Beecher's judgment on such a hazardous mission; so he confronted Beecher with his concern. The lieutenant looked his colonel in the eye, and replied: "Sir, from this day, John Barleycorn and I part company forever." It was a promise he kept for the few weeks he had left to live. This incident is related by Forsyth in "A Frontier Fight."

12 During a lull in the fighting, the embattled scouts had not only heard the sound of a bugle coming from the direction of the Indians, but also heard the remark, in perfect English: "There goes the last of their horses, anyway." It was undoubtedly the voice of a white man. Herbert Myrick, in his "The Mysterious Renegade (reprinted in the *The Beecher Island Annual*), opines that the remark was made by a renegade named "Kansas" to another white renegade, the bugler, a man known as "Nibsi." Both men had lived among the Cheyenne and had the confidence of the tribe. "Kansas" was actually John Clyborn, at one time a highly regarded soldier of the Seventh U. S. Cavalry, who had been captured by the Comanches and later traded to the Cheyenne. The artillery bugle had been taken by Roman Nose from a soldier in a previous battle. It was a proud possession of the chief, and he wanted the bugle sounded from time to time not only to stir his warriors but also to make sure that "Nibsi" had not left the Indians to fight with the scouts.

13 Troop H of the 10th Cavalry, which rescued the scouts, was under the command of Lieutenant Colonel L.H. Carpenter. The troop was an all-black unit known as "Carpenter's Brunettes."

14 Forsyth, "A Frontier Fight."

15 Mattes, "Battlefield Diary."

16 Letter from Shlesinger to Scout J.J. Peate and his comrades, *Beecher Island Annual*.

17 Fry, *Army and Navy Magazine*.

18 Document (no number), American Jewish Archives.

19 Letter from Shlesinger to Peate and comrades.

20 *Jewish Review and Observer*, Cleveland, April 27, 1928.

21 Ibid.

Chapter 2 Notes

1 Grant's two terms as president ran from 1869 to 1877. He took office at forty-six, died at sixty-three in 1886.

2 William S. McFeely, *Grant: A Biography*, (New York: W.W. Norton & Company, 1981), 289.

3   Ibid. 311.

4   Ibid. 308.

5   Ibid.

6   Henry G. Waltman, "Ely Samuel Parker," *The Commissioners of Indian Affairs*, ed. Robert M Krasnicka and Herman J. Viola (Lincoln: University of Nebraska Press, 1979), 123-33.

7   Ulysses S. Grant, *Memoirs and Selected Letters*:1 (New York: Literary Classics of the United States, 1990), p. 1133. On January 4, 1863, four days after he signed the final Emancipation Proclamation, Lincoln, in response to protests, revoked, through General Halleck, General Order 11, expelling Jews from the Department of Tennessee.

8   McFeely 307-08.

9   Ralph K. Andrist, *The Long Death* (New York: MacMillan, 1964), p

10 McFeely 307-08.

11 Ibid.

12 Ibid.

13 Ibid. 308-09.

14 Major General O.O. Howard *My Life and Experiences Among Our Hostile Indians* (Hartford: A.D. Worthington, n.d.), 122.

15 Waltman notes in "Ely Samuel Parker" that in the spring of 1869 politically chosen agents were replaced with sixty-eight "surplus" army officers, while eighteen Quakers were put in charge of tribes in Northern and Central superintendencies of the great plains.

16 McFeely 313.

17 William Brandon, *The American Heritage Book of Indians*, (New York: American Heritage Publishing Co., 1961), 360.

18 Ibid. 363.

19 Waltman 123-133.

20 McFeely 312.

21 Ibid. 309.

22 Ibid 123-24.

23 Norton B. Stern, "Herman Bendell: Superintendent of Indian Affairs, Arizona Territory, 1871-1873." *Western States Jewish History* (April, 1976), 265-282.

24 Ibid., quoting from Simon Wolf, *The Presidents I Have Known: 1860-1918* (Washington: Byron S. Adams Press, 1918), 80.

25 Letter to Herman Bendell from Office of Indian Affairs, January 17, 1871 *National Archives*, Record Group 75, Microcopy 21, Roll 100.

26 Waltman 123-133.

27 Jacob Rader Marcus, *Memoirs of American Jews: 1775-1865*:2 (Philadelphia: The Jewish Publication Society, 1955), 214. Simon Wolf was a Bavarian Jew who came to the United States at age twelve. He studied law in Cleveland and was admitted to the Ohio bar in 1861. He came to Washington the following year and remained there until his death in 1923.

28 Simon Wolf 80-81.

29 Ibid.

30 Stern, quoting from *The Voice of Israel*, San Francisco, Dec. 16, 1870, p. 5.

31 Ibid., quoting *Israel*, March 10, 1871, p. 21.

32 Stern 265-282.

33 *The New York Times*, November 15, 1932, p. 21.

34 Waltman 123-133.

35 McFeely 309.

36 Waltman 123-133.

37 Ibid.

38 McFeely 310.

39 Waltman 123-133.

40 Krasnicka and Viola xiii-xvi.

41 Edmund Jefferson Danziger, Jr. *Indians and Bureaucrats* (Urbana: University of Illinois Press, 1974), 206. When it was established in 1824, the Bureau of Indian Affairs was an agency of the War Department. It was subsequently transferred to the Department of the Interior. Over the years it has also been identified as The Indian Office, The Office, Indian Affairs, The Indian Bureau, and The Indian Department.

42 McFeely p. 13 notes that Indian agents received annual salaries of $1,500, but the potential for graft was enormous. For example, the Indians were dependent on the government for food, clothing, blankets and tools. The suppliers who paid the agents the most got the governmemt contract. An Episcopalian bishop, Henry B. Whipple, observed that it was "a tradition that an agent, paid a paltry $1,500, could retire upon an ample fortune in three years."

43 Stern, quoting the *Arizona Miner*, Prescott, May 20, 1871, p. 2.

44 Ibid, *Arizona Miner*, May 20, 1871, p. 2.

45 Letter from Bendell to Commissioner Parker, *National Archives*, Record Group 75, Microcopy 234, Roll 4.

46 Ibid.

47 Herman Bendell, "Annual Report to the Commissioner of Indian Affairs," August 22, 1871. *Western States Jewish History*:22, no.3, April, 1990 pp. 196-206. According to *What the Government and the Churches*

Are Doing For The Indians (Washington: U.S. Government Printing Office, 1874), 1873 expenditures of the various sects from their own treasuries for Indian missionary work were: Protestant Episcopal, $67,771.79; Presbyterian, $22,550.55.; Congregational, $3,300; Friends (northern and southern superintendencies), $17,500; Methodist, $5,000. Financial data are not available for Roman Catholic, Reformed Dutch, Lutheran or the Unitarian Church Society. In comparison, Bendell's annual appropriation in 1873 from the Indian Office for all tribes in his superintendency was $169,000.

48 *Arizona Miner,* June 7, 1873.

49 Waltman 123-133.

50 Ibid.

51 Ibid.

52 McFeely 314.

53 Waltman 123-133.

54 Ibid.

55 Ibid.

56 Ibid.

57 *Report of Honorable E.S. Parker, Commissioner of Indian Affairs to the Honorable Secretary of the Interior* (Columbus Delano) *On The Communication of William Welch, Esq., Relative to the Management of Indian Affairs.* (Washington: Joseph L. Pearson Printers, 1871).

58 Waltman 123-133.

59 Stern, quoting *The Jewish Times*, New York, January 6, 1871.

60 Ibid.

61 Simon Wolf 81-82.

62 Ibid.

63 Stern 265-285.

64 McFeely 315-16.

65 Waltman 123-133.

66 Robert M. Utley and Widicome E. Washburn *Indian Wars* (New York: American Heritage, 1985), 290.

67 Ibid.

68 Joel Nilsson, "Confusion Goes With Christianity," *Arizona Star,* June 3, 1973, p. 1.

Chapter 3 Notes

1   "Julius Meyer Ends His Own Life By Pistol Route," *Omaha World Herald*, May 12, 1909.

2   Ibid.

3   Ibid.

4   Ibid.

5   Alice Cromie, *Tour Guide to the Old West* (New York: Times Books, 1977), 238.

6   *World Herald* "Meyer Ends Life."

7   Charles M. Segal, "Curly Haired White Chief With One Tongue," *The National Jewish Monthly* n.d.

8   Ella Fleishman Auerbach, "The Austro-German Period of Settlement, 1863-1887," privately publ., Nebraska State Historical Society, 23-25.

9   Robert McMorris, "The People Who Make Up Omaha," *Omaha World Herald*, December 12, 1961.

10 *Historical and Descriptive Review of Omaha: Her Leading Business Houses and Enterprising Men*, Omaha, 1872. Nebraska State Historical Society.

11 Auerbach 23-25.

12 Susan Ludmer-Gilebe, "Box-Ka-Re-Sha-Hash-Ta-Ka From Nebraksa," *Toledo Jewish News*, July, 1929, p. 18.

13 Segal, *National Jewish Monthly*.

14 Ludmer-Gilebe, *Jewish News*.

15 McMorris, *World Herald*.

16 Segal, *National Jewish Monthly*.

17 Ibid.

18 *Illustrated History of Nebraska*:11, 1907, Nebraska State Historical Society.

19 James A. Hansen, "Laced Coats and Leather Jackets: The Great Plains Intercultural Clothing Exchange." In *Plains Indian Studies*, ed. Douglas H. Ubelaker and Herman J. Viola (Washington: Smithsonian Institution Press, 1982), 105-117.

20 Ibid.

21 Ibid.

22 Ibid.

23 Ibid. Hansen notes that the bullet-riddled bodies of a number of Custer's officers were recovered attired in Indian buckskin.

24 Carol Gendler, "The Jews of Omaha: The First Sixty Years," *Western States Jewish History*:5, no.3, April, 1973, pp. 205-266.

25 Segal, *National Jewish Monthly*.

26 Carolyn Thomas Foreman, *Indians Abroad: 1493-1938* (Norman: University of Oklahoma Press, 1943), p. 104-112.

27 Ibid.

28 Ibid.

29 "Descriptive Review of Omaha."

30 Ibid.

31 Ibid.

32 Ibid.

33 Gendler 205-266.

34 Auerbach 23-25.

35 *World Herald*, "Meyer Ends Life."

36 Ibid.

37 Ibid.

38 Ibid.

39 Interview with John Carter, Curator of Photography, Nebraska State Historical Society. It was Carter who brought to the attention of the author the photographs revealing Meyer to be right-handed.

40 *World Herald*, "Meyer Ends Life."

41 Ibid.

Chapter 4 Notes

1 The Pavants were a sub-tribe of the Utes, their name having been derived from their residence in the Pahvant Valley of Utah (Pah, water; vant, vanished).

2 Josiah F. Gibbs, "Gunnison Massacre 1853: Indian Mareer's Version of the Tragedy," *Utah Historical Quarterly*:1, no.3, Salt Lake City (July, 1928), 70.

3 Ibid.

4 Ibid.

5 Ibid.

6 Statement of Levi Abrams, August 29, 1855, Brigham Young's *Gubernatorial Letterbook*, p. 341, quoted in David Henry Miller, "The Impact of the Gunnison Massacre on Mormon-Federal Relations: Colonel Edward Jenner Steptoe's Command in Utah Territory, 1854-55." (Master's thesis University of Utah, 1968) 29-30.

7 Ibid.

8 Leon L. Watters, *The Pioneer Jews of Utah*, (New York: American Jewish

Historical Society, 1952), p. 25.

9   *Journal History*, Utah Historical Society Archives.

10 Very few Jews have become Mormons, as Juanita Brooks points out in
    The History of Jews in Utah and Idaho (Salt Lake City: Western Epics,
    1975), p. 30. The first convert was Alexander Neibauer, a Prussian
    dentist, who came to Nauvoo, Illinois, from England and set up his
    dental office in Brigham Young's front room. He became a Mormon in
    1838 and subsequently moved to Utah as one of Young's followers.
    Watters, p. 12, notes that Orson Hyde, one of the "Twelve Apostles" of
    the Mormon church, was a Jew, that same belief shared by Mormon
    authorities.

11 Brooks 31.

12 Leonard J. Arrington, *Brigham Young, American Prophet* (New York:
    Alfred A. Knopf, 1985), 126.

13 Miller 7.

14 Arrington 229.

15 William Chandless, *A Visit To Salt Lake* (London: Smith Elder & Co.,
    1857), 47-49.

16 Rev. C.P. Lyford, "Brigham Young's Record of Blood." Lecture
    delivered in the First M.E. church, Salt Lake City, January 23, 1876.
    Reprinted in the *Salt Lake Daily Tribune*, January 25, 1876.

17 Arrington 238.

18 Chandless 47-49.

19 Ibid.

20 Arrington 241.

21 Ibid. 210.

22 Ibid. 211.

23 Ibid.

24 Ibid. 212.

25 Ibid. 391.

26 Ibid. 216-17.

27 The peace treaty with Walkara was signed May, 1854. Solomon
    Carvalho had participated at the treaty in the company of Brigham
    Young and there had made sketches of Walkara and Kanosh for
    subsequent portraits of the chiefs.

28 Arrington 242.

29 Miller 2.

30 Ibid. 13.

31 John Charles Fremont conducted his own railroad survey at the same time as Gunnison. The Fremont expedition, which had no official sanction, explored a route farther to the south, through southern Utah, and was completed ahead of the Gunnison survey. Fremont's survey, however, received more attention than Gunnison's even though the Gunnison route was the one eventually chosen for the Union Pacific.

32 Miller 32.

33 Ibid. 6.

34 Gunnison was born in Goshen, New Hampshire, November 11, 1812. He married Martha A. Delaney of St. Mary's, Georgia, April 15, 1841. These and other biographical data are brought out by Nolie Mumie in *John Williams Gunnison: The Last of the Western Explorers* (Denver: Artcraft Press, 1955), 15.

35 Miller 11-12.

36 Miller quotes historian Herbert Howe Bancroft in *History of Utah* (San Francisco: The Horton Company, 1890) as describing Gunnison's book (Philadelphia: Lippincott Grambo & Co.) as "one of the most valuable and important works yet published by a gentile."

37 Miller 24.

38 Ibid.

39 Fillmore was the main community in Millard county. Both the county and the community itself were named for the thirteenth president.

40 Gibbs 70.

41 Ibid.

42 Miller 25.

43 Gibbs 71.

44 Gibbs 73-74.

45 Ibid.

46 Ibid.

47 Miller vi.

48 Ibid. viii.

49 Ibid. vii.

50 Judy W. Hanson, "The Gunnison Massacre: An Objective Overview." (Master's thesis University of Utah, n.d.) 28.

51 Gibbs (p.72) names the participants in the Gunnison massacre as Moshoquop; Pants; Mareer and his brother, Jim; Carboorits; Nunkiboolits; Tomwants and his son Koonants; Shipake; "Doctor" Jacob; Wabbits; Moab; Sam and his brother, Toady; Hunkootoops; Boquobits; and Jimmy Knights.

52 Miller 191-252.

53 Miller 206.

54 Hanson 29.

55 Ibid.

56 Miller 191-252.

57 Miller 210.

58 Brooks 32.

59 Arrington 233.

60 Ibid. 233-34.

61 Letter to Mrs. M.D. Gunnison from W.W. Drummond. "Narrative of the Death of Capt. Gunnison," Utah Historical Society, Salt Lake City, p. viii.

62 Brooks 32

63 Miller viii.

64 Ibid. 200.

65 Ibid. viii.

66 Letter from Mrs. Gunnison to Drummond, Utah Historical Society, p. viii.

67 Drummond to Mrs. Gunnison, Utah Historical Society, p. viii-xiv.

68 Ibid.

69 Jefferson Davis was undoubtedly the appropriate person to receive Young's document, but Young may also have believed that Davis would be a strong ally of his since both he and Davis were strongly pro-slavery.

70 Miller 191-271.

71 Arrington 247-271.

72 Ibid.

73 Ibid.

74 Ibid.

75 Ibid.

76 Ibid.

77 Mumie, *Last of Explorers*, 155.

78 Rev. C.P. Lyford.

79 Ibid.

80 John Hanson Beadle, *Life In Utah*, p. 172, quoted in Rev. C.P. Lyford.

81 Miller 23.

82 Ibid.

83 Sylvester Mowry, "The Mining States: How Should They Be Taxed?" Reprinted from *The New York Herald Tribune*, May, 1864.

84 *The Desert News Weekly* of February 2, 1881, reported that Judge Drummond had been observed in St. Louis, December 5, 1880 — "a man between sixty and seventy years of age, stoop-shouldered, seedy looking and wearing an air of general dejection." He was then employed as "a sewing machine agent." Jenson's *Church Chronology* later reported that Drummond "was sentenced to the house of correction for stealing postage stamps in Chicago, June 28, 1855; and on November 20, 1888 died a pauper in a grogshop in Chicago." Quoted in B. H. Roberts, *A Comprehensive History of the Church of Jesus Christ of Latter-day Saints*:9, p. 199.

85 Salt Lake City Directory, 1874.

86 Brigham Young's *Letterbook*, quoted in Arrington, p. 244.

Chapter 5 Notes

1 Joseph Sondheimer's obituary notice, published in an unidentified Guthrie, Oklahoma newspaper, is on file at The Thomas Gilcrease Museum, Tulsa. It places his arrival in Indian Territory at 1866. Another obituary, published July 11, 1913, in *The Muskogee Times-Democrat* also establishes his arrival date at 1866. However, Sondheimer himself, in correspondence with Chief Checote, recalls the date as 1877.

2 Samuel Sondheimer, "A Sketch of the Life and Career of Joseph Sondheimer," as told to Benjamin Martin, July 25, 1914. Oklahoma Historical Society Archives, Oklahoma City.

3 The Jews who came to Oklahoma between 1865 and 1885 were believed to be quite few. Those who may have arrived during these two decades may not have been identifiable as Jews because there were no Jewish congregations to help make known their identities.

4 Samuel Sondheimer "Sketch."

5 Personal observations by the author in Muskogee, Oklahoma, in 1983 and 1985. Beth Ahaba was located at 7th and Okmulgee until 1984 when the First Baptist Church of Muskogee made a property trade with the synagogue. It gave its property on Boston street to Beth Ahaba, building a new synagogue on the site as part of the agreement. In return, it took title to the more prominently located Okmulgee street property of Beth Ahaba. It is interesting to note that Beth Ahaba, which was founded in 1913, has never had enough members to warrant employing a permanent rabbi.

6   Author's observations.

7   Author's observations.

8   Archives of the First National Bank of Muskogee. Of interest: Robert L. Owen, who became one of the U.S. senators from Oklahoma, was one of the founders of the bank. It opened for business August 22, 1880, and is the oldest bank in Oklahoma.

9   O.A. Lambert, "Historical Sketch of Samuel Checote Once Chief of the Creek Nation." *Chronicles of Oklahoma*:4, p. 275. Oklahoma Historical Society.

10 Grant Foreman, "Oklahoma," *State Government Magazine*:19, no. 5, pp. 127-132.

11 Henry J. Tobias, *The Jews In Oklahoma* (Norman: University of Oklahoma Press, 1980).

12 Sondheimer obituary, Gilcrease Museum.

13 Samuel Sondheimer "Sketch."

14 "Railroads," *The Grant Foreman Papers*, Thomas Gilcrease Museum, Tulsa.

15 Ibid.

16 Ibid.

17 "The Last Fur Trader" *Kansas City Star*, October 29, 1903.

18 Sondheimer obituary, Guthrie, Oklahoma.

19 *Fur Trader.*

20 Ibid.

21 Ibid.

22 Ibid.

23 First National Bank Archives.

24 *Muskogee Phoenix*, January 21, 1892, p. 5. The reader should be mindful that Sondheimer's claim to the newspaper of selling "direct to the consumer" (thus eliminating the middleman) is a marketing claim that has echoed through the corridors of time. In can be viewed as being in sharp contrast to his claim to Chief Checote of being a wholesaler.

25 *Muskogee Phoenix*, March 24, 1892, p. 5.

26 "Indian Pioneer History," *Grant Foreman Collection*:14, p. 438. Oklahoma Historical Society.

27 Ibid.: 94, p. 367.

28 Ibid.: 60, p. 182.

29 Ibid.: 91, p. 381.

30 Personal interview with James B. Gibson, an early settler in Muskogee. Gibson, an attorney, served as a director of the First National Bank of Muskogee along with Samuel Sondheimer.

31 Personal interview with Joseph Sondheimer, grandson of the fur trader and son of Samuel Sondheimer. Sondheimer, who was born in Muskogee in 1918, resides in Glencoe, Illinois. He was born after his grandfather's death, and is not aware of any of the details surrounding the estrangement of his grandparents. He recalls, however, that his father would not speak of the incident. He recollects hearing that his grandmother died in his father's arms at the Brown Palace Hotel in Denver in 1919. Of further interest, the fur trader's wife, Johanna, had the same surname as her husband, and it is believed that they were cousins.

32 Petition to the city council, Wagoner, I.T., Oklahoma Historical Society Archives.

33 *Muskogee Phoenix,* January 21, 1892.

34 *Twin Territories*, November, 1900, p. 107.

35 Tobias, *Jews In Oklahoma*, notes that Alexander Sondheimer was born May 11, 1873, died August 20, 1923. His wife, Eudora Cobb Sondheimer was born March 4, 1874, died August 22, 1923. They are buried at Greenhill Cemetery in Muskogee.

36 F. M. Moore, *A Brief History of the Missionary Work in Indian Territory* (Muskogee: n.p., 1899), pp. 199-202.

37 O.A. Lambert 275-280.

38 F. M. Moore 199-202.

39 Ibid.

40 O.A. Lambert 275-280.

41 Grant Foreman, "Compilation of Confederate Records." *History of the Five Civilized Tribes in the Confederate Army.* Oklahoma Historical Society Archives.

42 O.A. Lambert 275-280.

43 Ibid.

44 Ibid.

45 Angie Debo, *The Road To Disappearance: A History of the Creek Indians* (Norman: University of Oklahoma Press, 1941) 199.

46 Ibid.

47 *The Indian Journal,* June 15, 1876. Oklahoma Historical Society Archives.

48 O.A. Lambert 275-280. Captain Frederick B. Severs joined the Confederate army, serving under Checote in a company of Creek full-bloods. He was the only white man in the company and subsequently was

adopted by the Creeks. He operated a trading post in Shiedville, I.T. after the war and later moved to Muskogee in 1868. In Muskogee he founded the Severs Hotel, the leading hostelry in town. It stands today but no longer operates.

49 Ibid.

50 "Permit Law of National Council of Muskogee Nation, 1900." File 39283, Oklahoma Historical Society Archives.

51 Ibid.

52 *The Indian Journal*, April 24, 1884. Files of First National Bank of Muskogee.

53 Document 39136, American Jewish Archives, Cincinnati.

54 Joseph Sondheimer in an interview remembers hearing that his grandfather had lost his stake because a partner had absconded with either funds or merchandise. The incident occurred while the fur trader resided in St. Louis, prior to his coming to Muskogee permanently in 1872. There is little doubt that the fur trader made back what he lost to his partner, and was financially stable at the time he wrote Checote, his protestation of "having lost all I possessed" notwithstanding. The presentation of "need" was very likely a strategy designed to arouse the sympathy of the chief. The Laupheimer brothers of Muskogee employed the same stragegy. (See note 57)

55 The Five Tribes had a body of men called "light horse," operating under the judicial branch of their governments. They served essentially as a mounted police force — "light horse" meaning lightly armed, highly mobile soldiers of the light cavalry. The term was originally used during the Revolutionary war in connection with General Henry Lee, better known as "Lighthorse Harry." One of the major duties of the light-horsemen was to serve as tax-collectors. Carolyn Foreman published a comprehensive study entitled "The Light Horse in Indian Territory," which appeared in *Chronicles of Oklahoma*: 34, no. 1, 1956.

56 Document 39147, American Jewish Archives.

57 Document 39177, American Jewish Archives, reveals that less than a year after Sondheimer's letter to Checote, the Laupheimer brothers wrote the chief protesting a tax increase from $100. to $200., the tax having been doubled within a year. Complaining bitterly, they wrote: "It is relly [sic] unjust to tax us that amount...we are paying cash and only the produce of the country and leave the money here. During the summer time we do not make expense...in our business, $100. tax would be a large tax. Consider the summer business." Checote made the following note on the Laupheimer letter: "Instruct LH Captain to collect $100. cash Ackl [sic] receipt and notify." Sondheimer, of course, was protesting paying any tax at all, the Laupheimers protesting only the amount.

58 File 39143, original manuscripts, "Creek Traders." Oklahoma Historical Society Archives.

59 Document 39148, American Jewish Archives.

60 O.A. Lambert 275-280.

61 Debo, 284.

62 Ibid.

63 O.A. Lambert 275-280.

64 *Muskogee Evening Times*, September 16, 1901.

65 *Muskogee Democrat*, March 7, 1904.

66 C. W. West *Muskogee: Queen City of the Southwest* (Muskogee: Muskogee Publishing Co., 1972), p. 59.

67 *Muskogee Times Democrat*, November 2, 1906.

68 "Fur Trader."

69 Foreman, "Oklahoma."

70 Ibid. It is ironic that the "Katy," with all the efforts to save itself at the expense of the Indians, nonetheless went broke in 1911.

71 Ibid. Perhaps the greatest irony of all is that the Seminoles who resisted removal in 1830 more strongly than any of the other Five Tribes and who also fought hardest against the Dawes Commission, ultimately became the wealthiest of the tribes as a result of oil discoveries on their alloted lands, lands far smaller in size than those of the other tribes.

72 Ibid.

73 Joseph Sondheimer interview, 1985.

74 Letter from Orlando Swain, The Creek Indian Memorial Association, to Mr. John B. Meserve, Tulsa, Oklahoma, Sept. 4, 1937. Oklahoma Historical Society Archives.

Chapter 6 Notes

1 Floyd Fierman, "The Impact of the Frontier on a Jewish Family: The Bibos," *American Jewish Historical Quarterly*:59, no. 4, (June 1970), 519.

2 Norton B. Stern, ed. *Western States Jewish History*, conducted an interview in 1969 with two of Bibo's children, LeRoy and Rose, and was told that their father spoke Navajo, Laguna and, mostly likely, Zuni, in addition to the Acoma tongue.

3 Ward Alan Minge, *Acoma: Pueblo In The Sky* (Albuquerque: University of New Mexico Press, 1976), 1.

4 Velma Garcia-Mason, "Acoma Pueblo," *Handbook of North American Indians*:9, ed. William C. Sturtevant (Washington: The Smithsonian Institution, 1979), 450.

5   Leslie A. White, "The Acoma Indians," *Fifty-Seventh Annual Report of the Bureau of American Ethnology* (Washington: The Smithsonian Institution, 1929-30), 25.

6   William Haworth, "The Country of Willa Cather," *National Geographic Magazine*:162, no.1 (July 1982), 89.

7   Garcia-Mason 450.

8   Charles F. Lummis, *The Land of Poco Tiempo* (Albuquerque: University of New Mexico Press, 1952), 30.

9   Garcia-Mason 460.

10 Minge 83.

11 Garcia-Mason 451.

12 Fierman 471.

13 Frank McNitt, *The Indian Traders* (Norman: University of Oklahoma Press, 1962), 116.

14 Floyd Fierman, *Impact of the Frontier* (El Paso: Texas Western Press, 1961), p. 18. This is an earlier edition, with a less complete text, than that published by the *American Jewish Historical Society*. See note 1.

15 "30 year lease pueblo of Acoma to Solomon Bibo," New Mexico State Records Center and Archives, Santa Fe, NM.

16 Ibid.

17 Sandra Lea Rollins, "Jewish Indian Chief," *Western States Jewish History*:1, no.4 (July, 1969) 160.

18 Ibid.

19 Herbert O. Brayer, *Pueblo Indian Land Grants of the Rio Abajo, New Mexico*. University of New Mexico Bulletin No. 334. (Albuquerque: University of New Mexico Press, 1938), 14.

20 Ibid. 10.

21 Ibid. 9.

22 Ibid. 18.

23 Ibid. 22.

24 Ibid. 23.

25 Minge 58.

26 Ibid.

27 Ibid.

28 Fierman, Texas Western edition 14.

29 McNitt 118.

30 Ibid.

31 Ibid. 119

32 Ibid.

33 Ibid.

34 Ibid. 121.

35 Ibid.

36 Ibid.

37 Rollins 161.

38 Fierman, *Jewish Historical Society* edition, p. 475.

39 McNitt 121.

40 Fierman 475-476.

41 Ibid.

42 Brayer 25.

43 Correspondence with Carl Bibo, June 1, 1983. The Bibo daughters were Rose (1887-1976); Clara (1890-1953); Celia (1894-1924); and Irma (1896-). LeRoy Isaac Bibo, the eldest son, was born in 1899, died in 1976. Carl David Bibo, born in 1911, is a retired letter carrier residing in Santa Fe.

44 Ibid.

45 Ibid.

Chapter 7 Notes

1 S. N. Carvalho, *Incidents of Travel and Adventure in the Far West with Colonel Fremont's Last Expedition Across The Rocky Mountains* (New York: Derby & Jackson, 1860), 108.

2 Ibid. 18.

3 Ibid. 17-18.

4 Ferol Egan, *Fremont, Explorer For A Restless Nation*, (Garden City: Doubleday & Co.), 491-524.

5 Ibid. 491-524.

6 Bertram W. Korn, "Some Additional Notes on the Life and Works of Solomon Nunes Carvalho," *Jewish Quarterly Review, Seventy-Fifth Anniversary Volume*, Philadelphia, 1967.

7 Carvalho 38.

8 Egan 491-524.

9 Juanita Brooks, *The History of the Jews in Utah and Idaho* (Salt Lake City: Western Epics, 1973), 18.

10 Egan 491-524.

11 Carvalho 22.

12 Egan 491-524.

13 Ibid.

14 Ibid.

15 Ibid.

16 Carvalho 62-64.

17 Ibid.

18 Ibid. 46.

19 Ibid. 47.

20 Ibid. 65.

21 Ibid. 36.

22 Ibid. 54-55.

23 Ibid. 37.

24 Ibid. 67-68.

25 Ibid.

26 Ibid. 69-70.

27 Ibid. 71.

28 Ibid. 82-83.

29 Egan 491-524.

30 Carvalho 87.

31 Ibid. 108.

32 Ibid. 110.

33 Ibid. 120.

34 Ibid. 130.

35 Egan 491-524.

36 Carvalho 143.

37 Brooks 18.

38 Ibid. 3.

39 Carvalho 46.

40 Ibid. 156.

41 Ibid.

42 Ibid. 157.

43 Ibid. 181.

44 Ibid. 180.

45 Ibid. 183.

46 Ibid. 187.

47 Ibid. 188.

48 Ibid.

49 Ibid. 189.

50 Ibid.

51 Ibid. 190.

52 Ibid. 191-92.

53 Ibid.

54 Ibid. 193.

55 Ibid. 197.

56 Ibid. 198.

57 Ibid. 208.

58 Ibid. 211-12.

59 Quoted in Korn, "Additional Notes."

60 Egan 491-524.

61 Ibid.

62 Korn, "Additional Notes."

63 "Rabbi Bertram Korn Papers," American Jewish Archives, Cincinnati. Solomon Carvalho's brother, Emmanuel, was born in Charleston, March 22, 1817, and died in New York, March 13, 1883. Emmanuel married Caroline A. Wolfe, December 1, 1841. She lived until March 9, 1904. Solomon's sister, Julia, was born July 4, 1819, died in New York, January 22, 1887, never having married. His sister, Sarah, was born in 1823, died in the Barbados at age nineteen.

64 Isaac Markens, *The Hebrews In America* (New York: Self Published, 1888).

65 Korn, "Additional Notes."

66 Ibid.

67 Ibid.

68 Joan Sturhahn, *Carvalho, Artist, Photographer, Adventurer, Patriot: Portrait of a Forgotten American* (Merrick, New York: Richwood Publishing Co., 1976). This most definitive study of Carvalho's life and works offers a penetrating evaluation of Carvalho's paintings. The author is Carvalho's great-granddaughter, and she was able to track down the originals of forty-seven Carvalho paintings and seven daguerreotypes. Another fourteen paintings together with daguerreotypes of the fifth Fremont expedition have not been located.

69 "In Memoriam," *The American Hebrew*:61, no.5, June 4, 1897.

70 Sturhahn 32.

71 *The Occident*:10, no.3, June, 1852, p. 174. American Jewish Archives.

72 Ibid.:3, no.8, November, 1845, p. 420.

73 Letter from S.N. Carvalho to Solomon Solis, Esq., undated. American Jewish Archives, Cincinnati.

74 "Rabbi Bertram Korn Papers." Solomon's eldest son, David, was born in Philadelphia, September 29, 1848. He married Annie Abrams, March 22, 1878. There were six children of this union. David, like his father, was a man of accomplishment. He was a renowned handwriting expert and the ultimate authority on the age and composition of ink. He was the author of *Fifty Centuries of Ink* (New York: 1904), and a master in the detection of forgeries. His testimony relating to the falsity of documents used in the conviction of Alfred Dreyfus in France were reportedly instrumental in the latter's acquittal. He died in 1925. Charity Solis, the second eldest child, was born in Baltimore, April 12, 1850, died in New Rochelle, New York, April 5, 1945. She and her husband, Adolph Marshuetz, a Bavarian immigrant, had five children. Charity was a loving daughter and cared for her father, Solomon, during his three surviving years as a widower. The third child, Jacob Solis, was born in Charleston, September 23, 1852, died in Lawrence, Long Island, March 12, 1909. He was married to Suzanne Walker who lived until 1941. Jacob was president of a lumber company in New York. Solomon Solis, the youngest of the artist's children, was born in Baltimore, January 16, 1856, died April 12, 1942. Solomon had a distinguished career as a newspaper man. He had been associated with *The New York Sun* and *The New York World* and later had become general manager of the Hearst publications.

75 Egan 491-524.

76 Letter to an unidentified relative from Carvalho's nephew, September 11, 1856. American Jewish Archives.

77 Ibid.

78 Egan 491-524.

79 Ibid.

80 Ibid.

81 Ibid.

82 Ibid.

Works Cited

Andrist, Ralph K. *The Long Death*. New York: MacMillan, 1964.

Arrington, Leonard J. *Brigham Young: American Moses*. New York: Alfred A. Knopf, 1985.

Brandon, William. *The American Heritage Book of Indians*. New York: American Heritage, 1961.

Brayer, Herbert O. *Pueblo Indian Land Grants of the Rio Abajo, New Mexico*. University of New Mexico Bulletin. Albuquerque: University of New Mexico Press, 1938.

Brooks, Juanita. *The History of the Jews in Utah and Idaho*. Salt Lake City: Western Epics, 1973.

Carvalho, S. N. *Incidents of Travel and Adventure in the Far West with Col. Fremont's Last Expedition Across the Rocky Mountains*. New York: Derby & Jackson, 1860.

Chandless, William. *A Visit to Salt Lake City: Being a Journey Across the Plain and a Residence in the Mormon Settlements of Utah*. London: Smith, Elder & Co., 1857.

Cromie, Alice. *Tour Guide to the Old West*. New York: Times Books, 1977.

Danziger, Edmund Jefferson, Jr. *Indians and Bureaucrats*. Urbana: University of Illinois Press, 1974.

Debo, Angie. *The Road to Disappearance*. Norman: University of Oklahoma Press, 1941.

Egan, Ferol. *Fremont, Explorer for a Restless Nation*. Garden City: Doubleday & Co., 1977.

Fierman, Floyd S. *The Impact of the Frontier on a Jewish Family: The Bibos*. El Paso: Texas Western College Press, 1961.

Foreman, Carolyn Thomas. *Indians Abroad: 1493-1938*. Norman: University of Oklahoma Press, 1943.

Garcia-Mason, Velma. "Acoma Pueblo." In *Handbook of North American Indians, Southwest*. vol.9, pp. 450-466. Edited by William C. Sturtevant. Washington: The Smithsonian Institution, 1979.

Grant, Ulysses S. *Memoirs and Selected Letters*. vol.1. New York: Literary Classics of the United States, 1990.

Hansen, James A. "Laced Coats and Leather Jackets: The Great Plains Intercultural Clothing Exchange." In *Plains Indian Studies*, pp. 106-117. Edited by Douglas H. Whitaker and Herbert Viola. Washington: Smithsonian Institution, 1982.

Howard, General O.O. *My Life and Experiences Among Our Hostile Indians*. Hartford, A.D. Worthington _____.

Waltman, Henry G. "Ely Samuel Parker." In *The Commisssioners of Indian Affairs 1824-1977*. Edited by Robert M. Krasnicka and Herman J. Viola. Lincoln: University of Nebraska Press, 1979.

Lummis, Charles F. *The Land of Poco Tiempo*. Albuquerue: University of New Mexico Press, 1952.

Marcus, Jacob Rader. *Memoirs of American Jews: 1775-1865*. Vol.2. Philadelphia: The Jewish Publication Society of America, 1955.

Markens, Isaac. *The Hebrews in America*. New York: By the author, 1888.

Minge, Ward Alan. *Acoma: Pueblo in the Sky*. Alburquerque: University of New Mexico Press.

McFeely, William S. *Grant: A Biography*. New York: W.W. Norton & Co., 1981.

McNitt, Frank. *The Indian Traders*. Norman: University of Oklahoma Press, 1962.

Moore, F. M. *A Brief History of the Missionary Work in Indian Territory*. Muskogee: _____, 1899.

Mumey, Nolie. *John Williams Gunnison (1812-1853): The Last of the Western Explorers*. Denver: Artcraft Press, 1955.

Sturhahn, Joan: *Carvalho: Artist, Photographer, Adventurer, Patriot: Portrait of a Forgotten American*. Merrick, N.Y., Richwood Publishing Co., 1976.

Tobias, Henry J. *The Jews In Oklahoma*. Norman: Oklahoma University Press, 1980.

Utley, Robert M. and Washburn, Widicombe E. *Indian Wars*. New York: American Heritage, 1985.

Watters, Leon L. *The Pioneer Jews of Utah*. New York: American Jewish Historical Society, 1952.

West, C. W. *Muskogee: Queen City of the Southwest.* Muskogee: Muskogee Publishing Co., 1972.

White, Leslie A. "The Acoma Indians." In *Fifty-Seventh Annual Report of the Bureau of American Ethnology.* Washington: Smithsonian Institution, 1929-39.

Wolf, Simon. *Presidents I Have Known, 1866-1918.* Washington, Byron S. Adams Press, 1918.

Periodicals

Brady, Cyrus Townsend. "Carpenter and His Brunettes. In *Beecher Island Annual.* 5. Edited by Robert Lynam. Wray, Colorado: Beecher Island Battle Memorial Association, 1917.

Foreman, Grant. "Oklahoma." *State Government Magazine* 19. (May, 1946).

Foreman, Carolyn Thomas. "The Light-Horse in the Indian Territory." 34. *Chronicles of Oklahoma.* (Spring, 1956). Oklahoma Historical Society.

Forsyth, General George A. "A Frontier Fight." In *Beecher Island Annual.* 5. Edited by Robert Lynam. Wray, Colorado: Beecher Island Battle Memorial Association, 1917.

Gendler, Carol. "The Jews of Omaha: The First Sixty Years." *Western States Jewish History* 5. (April, 1973).

Gibbs, Josiah F. "Gunnison Massacre 1853: Indian Mareer's Version of the Tragedy." *Utah Historical Quarterly* 1. (July 1928).

Historical and Descriptive Review of Omaha: Her Leading Business Houses and Enterprising Men. Nebraska State Historical Society (January, 1872).

Korn, Bertram W. "Some Additional Notes on the Life and Works of Solomon Nunes Carvalho." *Jewish Quarterly Review: Seventy Fifth Anniversary Volume.* (1967).

Lambert, O.A. "Historical Sketch of Col. Samuel Checote, Once Chief of the Creek Nation." *Chronicles of Oklahoma.* 4. Oklahoma Historical Society.

Mattes, Merrill J. "The Beecher Island Battlefield Diary of Sigmund Shlesinger." *Colorado Magazine.* (July, 1952).

Myrick, Herbert. "The Mysterious Renegade." In *Beecher Island Annual.* 5. Edited by Robert Lynam. Wray, Colorado, Beecher Island Battle Memorial Association, 1917.

Rollins, Sandra Lea. "Jewish Indian Chief." *Western States Jewish History.* 1 (July, 1969).

Stern, Norton B. "Herman Bendell: Superintendent of Indian Affairs, Arizona Territory, 1871-1873." *Western States Jewish History.* (April, 1976).

Segal, Charles M. "Curly Haired White Chief With One Tongue." *National Jewish Monthly* (____).

Siegel, Burt A. "The Little Jew Was There." *American Jewish Archives.* 20. (April, 1968).

Collections, Reports, Theses

Bendell, Herman. "Annual Report to the Commissioners of Indian Affairs." Cited by Norton B. Stern, Editor, *Western States Jewish History.* 22. (1990).

Foreman, Grant. "Compilations of Confederate Records." In *History of the Five Civilized Tribes in the Confederate Army.* Oklahoma Historical Society (_____).

Foreman, Grant. "Indian Pioneer History." *Grant Foreman Collection: Oral History Transcripts.* 14. Oklahoma Historical Society.

Hanson, Judy. W. "The Gunnison Massacre: An Objective Overview." Master's Thesis, University of Utah, _____.

Miller, David Henry. "The Impact of the Gunnison Massacre on Mormon-Federal Relations: Colonel Edward Jenner Steptoe's Command in Utah Territory: 1854-1855. Master's Thesis, University of Utah, 1968.

Parker, Eli Samuel. *Report of Commissioner of Indian Affairs to the Hon. Secretary of the Interior on the Communications of William Welch, Esq. Relative to the Management of Indian Affairs.* Washington: Joseph L. Pearson, Printers, 1870.

What the Government and the Churches are Doing for the Indians. Washington: U.S. Government Printing Office, 1874.

Index

L

Labatt, S.K. 145
Laguna pueblo 114, 116, 119, 121
Lamar, Colo. 137
Lambert, O.A. 102
Laupheimer brothers *166*
Laupheimer, Elias 101
Laupheimer, Harry 101
Lawrence, Kans. 4
Lazard, S. 145
Leavenworth, Kans. 15
Lee, General Robert E. 31
Leeser, Isaac 147, 150
Leipzig, Germany 90
Levi, Herman 6
Levi, Joseph 6
Lewi, Wilhelmine 45
Lewis, Merriwether 54, 55
Lighthorse Harry 166
Lighthorse Man 98
Lillie, Gordon W. (Pawnee Bill) 56
Lincoln, Abraham 128, 146, 149, 150
Liptrott, Private 64, 70
Little Big Horn 55
Little River, (I.T.) 94
Little Robe, Chief 21
Little Salt Lake Valley 139
London Ecumenical Conference 102
Los Angeles 141, 144, 145, 146
Los Angeles River 147
Lost Tribes of Israel 6
Lummis, Charles F. 111, 125
Lutherans 33

M

Manti, Utah 70
Marks, Manfred
 (father) 3, 4, 5, 7, 9, 10
Marmon, Robert 121
Marmon, Walter 121
Marshuetz, Adolph *172*
Max Meyer & Bro. Co. 51, 52, 56
McCarty's 108, 120, 121
McCormick, Richard C. 36
McFeely, William S. 35
McKinley, William 103
McNitt, Frank 123
Meadow Creek 62, 64, 70
Mears, Otto 6
Memphis, Tenn. 88
"Mericats" 62, 67, 74, 79, 80
Merteens, Private 64, 70
Methodism 93, 102

Methodist church 93, 94
Methodist Episcopal Church, South 94, 102
Methodist North Fork circuit 94
Mexican rule (pueblos) 109, 117
Mexico 117, 118
Meyer, Adolph 51, 56, 57
Meyer brothers 51, 56, 57
Meyer, Julius 5, 49-59 (see Box-Ka-Re-Sha-Hash-Ta-Ka) 51, 52, 56, 57
Meyer, Max 51, 52, 56, 57
Meyer, Moritz 49, 51, 52, 56-58
Midsummer 74
Millard County Blade 71
Millard County, Utah 70
Mills, Lieutenant Stephen 55
Minnimmuck, Chief 21
Mississippi River 29, 68, 84, 105
Missouri 63, 64
Missouri, Kansas and Texas Railroad
 (the "Katy") 84, 88, 89, 104
Missouri River 79
Mooers, J. H. 21, 25
Mormons (Church of Jesus Christ of Latter-day Saints) 6, 61-81, 132, 139, 143, 144
Mormon church 61-81, 141, *160*
Mormon Minute Men 79
Mormon rolls 63
Mormon-Federal War 64
Mormon-Indian War 63
"Mormonees" 62, 67, 69, 80
Mormons as Jews 64
Morphy, Paul 147
Morris, Captain R.M. 68, 70
Morse, Samuel F. B. 129
Moshoquop, Chief 62, 70, 71, 73
Mount Sinai cemetery (St. Louis) 105
Mountain Department 150
Mountain Meadows massacre 79, 80
Mowrey, Lieutenant Sylvester 73, 76, 81
Mowrey silver mines 81
Muskogee Embroidery Club 93
Muskogee Evening Times 102
Muskogee nation 98, 99
Muskogee, Okla. 9, 83-105
Muskogee Times-Democrat 103

N

Napoleon 113
National Congress of American Indians 48
National Jewish Monthly 55